"With compassion, clarity [...] the reader through a refreshing look at how God's grace in Christ is the most important antidote for anxiety and depression. As I read *Down, Not Out*, I found myself growing in compassion for so many people I know who struggle in significant ways. Chris offers a personal, gracious God who walks with us, encourages us, and provides hope and comfort along the path. Each carefully written chapter exudes comfort and hope. I can't think of anyone who doesn't need that!"

DR TIMOTHY LANE, *President, Institute for Pastoral Care*

"This book is beautifully straightforward, deeply honest and consistently profound. Chris Cipollone not only gives us a gentle yet compelling insight into the world of depression and anxiety, but consistently and winsomely points us to the Lord Jesus Christ, in whom real and ultimate answers are to be found. It may not take long to read this book, but the time invested will change the way you think about and respond to mental-health issues, whether in your own life, your family or the church."

GARY MILLAR, *Principal, Queensland Theological College*

"For followers of Christ who live with mental illness, this book acknowledges the reality and pain of that suffering, and points to the sweet solace that can be found in our gospel identity."

TANYA LING, *blogger at GoThereFor.com and patientreflections.wordpress.com*

"Chris has written a book the church needs. The result is winsome and wise biblical counsel which honours Christ profoundly and will help sufferers and carers alike. I've already been helped; now I'll be using this book, and commending it widely."

DR ANDREW NICHOLLS, *Director of Pastoral Care, Oak Hill College*

"Chris 'gets' mental illness. He has been in the dark places and openly shares his personal experience. We hear of the help that can be gained from medical and psychological treatments, and the difference that a supportive community can make. But with a pastor's heart, Chris's main aim is to speak biblical truth into this difficult context—to gently correct false patterns of thinking and feeling, and above all, to point the reader to the joy and refreshment that is found in knowing that our acceptance, security and hope depend upon God's unchanging love, not the quality of our mental health."

KEITH CONDIE, *Co-Director, Mental Health and Pastoral Care Institute, Anglican Deaconess Ministries, Sydney, Australia*

"Mental health is an important issue that is often overlooked or misunderstood in the church. *Down, Not Out* is a step in the right direction—an encouraging book for those of us suffering from anxiety and depression, and a helpful guide for those who do not." **ADAM FORD,** *Founder, The Babylon Bee*

"*Down, Not Out* is a wonderfully helpful book for anyone struggling with mental illness or seeking to better love and understand those who face this challenge. God's immense kindness, faithfulness and goodness in Christ is powerfully proclaimed throughout. I wholeheartedly commend this book and the truth therein that Jesus makes the ultimate difference to depression and anxiety."

LILY STRACHAN, *Australian Fellowship of Evangelical Students*

"Chris Cipollone combines insightful intelligence with the real grit of lived experience to bring perspective and hope to those living with mental-health difficulties."

JOHN BURNS, *Clinical Psychologist*

CHRIS CIPOLLONE

DOWN
NOT OUT

Down Not Out

© Chris Cipollone/The Good Book Company, 2018

Published by:
The Good Book Company
Tel (US): 866 244 2165
Tel (UK): 0333 123 0880
Email (US): info@thegoodbook.com
Email (UK): info@thegoodbook.co.uk

Websites:
North America: www.thegoodbook.com
UK: www.thegoodbook.co.uk
Australia: www.thegoodbook.com.au
New Zealand: www.thegoodbook.co.nz

Unless indicated, all Scripture references are taken from the HOLY BIBLE, NEW INTERNATIONAL VERSION. Copyright © 2011 Biblica, Inc.™ Used by permission.

ISBN: 9781784981419 | Printed in the UK

Design by André Parker | Cover design by ninefootone creative

CONTENTS

INTRODUCTION
WELCOME

Thanks for picking up this book. We hope you find it helpful. In it we will look at the pain of mental illness, especially depression and anxiety. And we will raise some difficult questions, especially asking what it means for a Christian to live with these illnesses.

Both of us have experienced the pain of depression over many years, so we know first-hand what that struggle is like. Our hope and prayer is that we can serve you well, whether you experience mental illness yourself or are caring for someone who does. We want to give hope and encouragement, as we look together at the difference Jesus makes to those of us who are depressed or anxious. Our belief is that our gospel identity—as loved and forgiven children of God—transforms our experience of these difficult and unwanted illnesses.

But we also want to ask you, please, to take care of yourself. It may well be that the pages of this book raise painful issues for you, maybe even for the first time. If so, please don't struggle alone. One of the joys for any Christian is that they have been adopted into God's family. We have brothers and sisters in Christ. So if the themes of this book cause you to struggle, please turn to a pastor, counsellor or trusted Christian friend for help. Alternatively, you will find a list of supportive organisations at the end of this book.

As we have worked on this book together, we have prayed for those who will read it. Our prayer is that your hope in Jesus will grow as he shows you how your identity in him transforms every area of your life.

Chris Cipollone *(author)*
and Alison Mitchell *(editor)*

CHAPTER 1
THIRTY

My story

My blood pressure had dropped from its normal 120/80 to 90/50. I'm no doctor, but even I know that's not good. I'm sure the unseasonable warmth of a sunny September day was not the main reason I'd collapsed. Rather, it was the climax of the days, weeks, months and years leading up to that moment.

It was the morning of September 23, 2014. In three days' time, I would be turning 30. I had two children under the age of 3 and a wife who loved me, and I was literally weeks away from completing my theological training. I had an offer to join the pastoral team of a church, and the deadline for a decision was looming. I had just completed a personal training session in which I had pushed myself too far, and now I found myself lying on the floor.

Lying on the floor of a psychiatric hospital.

It wasn't meant to be like this. Turning 30 should have been momentous for so many reasons, but this shouldn't have been one of them. Instead of celebrating with my kids and enjoying breakfast in bed, I would wake up to a nurse and pills.

My twenties had been a time of great change—graduation from university, the beginning of a career, marriage, parenthood, multiple house moves and entry into vocational ministry. Through it all, career choices had become my greatest anxiety. On the cusp of another life-change, I couldn't cope. What if I made the wrong decision? What if I was heading down a path that was not well suited to me? Shouldn't I have felt validated in the "call" to ministry? Instead, I was crippled.

In the years leading up to this, I had been on and off medication, in and out of psychologists' offices. In the week prior to my admission to hospital, I walked around my neighbourhood at 3am, sure that God would give me an answer. Instead, all I felt was further turmoil. I knew I needed more medical help than I'd received to that point. Life was impossible, and in my mind, it was no longer worth living with this kind of pain. Perhaps you have felt like this as well.

Seasons

A friend once introduced me to the idea that life is made up of seasons, each with its own joys and challenges. Some seasons are marked by change, others by stability.

It made me think of a song I first heard at my grandparents' house as a young boy. That song was "Turn! Turn! Turn!" by The Byrds. It's a song that says there's a time for everything. What I didn't realise until later in my walk with God was that the words came from the Bible:

There is a time for everything,
and a season for every activity under the heavens:

A time to be born and a time to die,
A time to plant and a time to uproot,
A time to kill and a time to heal,
A time to tear down and a time to build,
A time to weep and a time to laugh,
A time to mourn and a time to dance,
A time to scatter stones and a time to gather them,
A time to embrace and a time to refrain from embracing,
A time to search and a time to give up,
A time to keep and a time to throw away,
A time to tear and a time to mend,
A time to be silent and a time to speak,
A time to love and a time to hate,
A time for war and a time for peace.

ECCLESIASTES 3 V 1-8

The years leading up to this lowest of points in my life seemed like one long season of tearing down. There was very little building or planting, but rather, what felt like constant uprooting. Laughing and dancing had made way for weeping and mourning.

Since graduating from university, anxiety about what to do next had plagued me. I initially trained as a teacher, and worked quite happily in the classroom for a number of years. But I worried about how long I could remain in the profession. So I considered any possible career you could imagine: doctor, marketing executive, carpenter, gelato-maker, pilot, psychologist, sporting coach. The list went on and on, and so did the days I fretted about it.

After much agonising, my wife, Lara, and I decided I should go to Bible college. Given the anxieties that had led up to the moment, I'm not going to give a romanticised picture of receiving a calling to go. All I knew was that what I felt most strongly about in this life was the gospel. I was passionate about sharing my faith with others.

And so I went. Some see Bible college as a route to-wards church ministry. I didn't see it that way. I could also envisage myself in school chaplaincy, or maybe a not-for-profit organisation, or even academia. I was sure I'd know at the end of the three years of training which avenue God had placed before me. So here I was, after a long season in the wilderness, waiting for a clear path.

And it wasn't coming.

I felt as if I'd wandered through the desert. Not for 40 years, but for at least five years since growing discon-tent with my teaching career. I thought this would be the time when I'd peer over the mountain, and gaze out at what was set before me. Instead, I had become a ball of anxiety, unable to know which way to go.

A diagnosis

In time, what I thought was anxiety a psychiatrist diagnosed as depression. The two often go hand in hand. The reason I couldn't work out what to do was because I couldn't help but see the negative in everything. Nothing was appealing because life itself had become impossible to enjoy. When I thought about being a doctor, all I could think of was the oppressive training involved. When I thought about being a pilot, I could only see the financial costs. And when I thought about carpentry, the toll on my body was too much to imagine.

For the final 12 months of my Bible-college training, the church I was working at as a student minister was keen for me to come on board at the end of the year. In my depression, I couldn't see the positive in the situation— but of course no other option seemed any different. In my depression, everything seemed hopeless.

For the reader

Perhaps you are reading this book because you live with mental illness. If so, it is my hope and prayer that my story will encourage you to see that your faith in Christ can make a dramatic difference in how you navigate your life. My story does get better, and so can yours.

Don't hear me over-promising. I still live with depression. But life has seasons, and in God's grace it is possible to press on. Your life has dignity because God gave it to you. Read this book at your own pace. It's intentionally written in short chapters so you can digest as much, or as little, as you can cope with.

Maybe you're reading this book because you care deeply about someone who is suffering from mental illness. If that is you, thank you. Thank you that you care deeply enough to offer an outstretched hand. I should warn you that it's likely there will be times when your offers of help will not be wanted or appreciated. You will probably do or say the wrong thing. Please rest in God's grace and keep loving that person, whoever they may be.

Maybe you don't know of anyone who is presently suffering, but you're learning of the effects and extent of mental illness. For you, I hope this book helps you better understand what mental illness looks like, particularly for the servant of Christ.

Or maybe you have reservations about mental illness, doubting its legitimacy. If this is you, can I assure you that depression and anxiety are real. Thank you for picking up this book, and I would encourage you to approach it with an open mind.

I'm aware that this is my story, and that the stories of others will be very different. Depression and anxiety are as individual as those who live with them. But no matter what the life circumstances, causes, manifestations or treatments, I know that in the gospel we have one identity in Jesus Christ—and so I hope for this reason that the pages of this book prove useful for all who read them.

A gospel identity

Throughout this book, I will come back to the idea that, as Christians, we have a "gospel identity". What do I mean by this? In the gospel, we have victory over sin, death and the devil. This victory is achieved for us through Christ's death and resurrection, in spite of our own sin.

This truth leads us to rightly conclude that God loves us more than we could imagine. When we experience dark times and feel as though God doesn't care, we must come back to the fact that he has not even spared his own Son in pursuit of us. Our identities are not as depressives, or the anxious. We are not defined by bipolar, schizophrenia or addiction. These may all be significant parts of our journey through life, but they are not at the core of who we are. Rather, we are beloved children of God, and this, more than any other truth, must impact how we navigate mental illness.

> *See what great love the Father has lavished on us, that we should be called children of God! And that is what we are!*   I JOHN 3 V I

For reflection

The beauty of the gospel is that, even at our lowest, we are more than our illness. If we are in Christ, then our identity is secure in him. This helps us to process and grow through all seasons.

CHAPTER 2
BROKENNESS

It's amazing how often we convince ourselves that we are independent, self-made people. Our families, our careers, our homes and our cars can so easily become the objects of our own creation. At least in our minds.

We work hard; we play hard; we spend hard. The world is ours for the taking.

But mental illness can often remove the ability to function well in society. Days at work are replaced by days in bed, and our sense of security is taken away.

In the lead-up to my stay in hospital, I simply couldn't cope anymore. I couldn't face my ministry responsibilities at church or the deadlines that loomed for college. I couldn't enjoy my children or appreciate my marriage. My bed became my refuge, and I didn't want to leave.

Light in the darkness

On that day when I found myself lying on the floor of the hospital, God reached out to me with immense clarity.

In that moment, I had no security in the things of this world. I didn't know how I would complete my studies. I wasn't sure when I would be able to return to work, how I was going to pay my mortgage, or whether I was ever going to be the same again.

But something amazing happened in that moment as well. I realised that for all that had been taken away on account of my mental illness, one thing had not been snatched from me, and that was the love of Christ.

As I came back to consciousness and my blood pressure rose to a normal level, the words of a song came rushing into my mind. "Desert Song", by Hillsong United, repeats these simple lines a number of times:

All of my life, in every season
You are still God, I have a reason to sing
I have a reason to worship[1]

It was truly an act of grace that God put these words in my heart and on my mind at that moment. I couldn't move my body, but a small smile came across my face. Everything had been stripped away. I was a shell of a person on the outside, and yet God had not changed. Even then, I had a reason to sing—a reason to worship.

My peace I give you

I have no doubt that this was the Holy Spirit speaking to me. God the Holy Spirit performs many functions. Scripture reveals that one of these is to remind believers of all that God the Son has said. As Jesus was preparing to depart from this world and his disciples, he left his closest friends with these words:

> *But the Advocate, the Holy Spirit, whom the Father will send in my name, will teach you all things and will remind you of everything I have said to you. Peace I leave with you; my peace I give you. I do not give to you as the world gives. Do not let your hearts be troubled and do not be afraid.*   JOHN 14 V 26-27

Jesus tells his disciples not to be troubled or afraid. He knows they will face significant hardship in their lives. But God the Holy Spirit will remind them of all he has said. The truth is that Jesus said many things, but the heart of his message is that his love runs so deep that he gave himself for us. We will be reminded that he is the way, the truth and the life—and that no one comes to the Father except through him (John 14 v 6).

In that moment on the floor, when I felt the most unloveable, the Holy Spirit reminded me of just how loved I was. God was still God, and for that reason I still had a reason to sing and a reason to worship.

The Holy Spirit gave me that peace in my most desperate hour. My gospel identity became clearer to me than ever before. I wasn't Chris the teacher, Chris the theologian or Chris the father. I was Chris the child of God.

In that moment, I couldn't prove anything to anyone. I couldn't prove whether I'd be able to function the way I wanted to. But in the gospel, there is nothing left to prove because God loves us—not because of what we can provide, but through the salvation Christ offers. God has given us everything we ever need, and it has nothing to do with our own abilities or performance.

In his mercy, God chose me to be a child of his, and in his continuing desire to show me mercy, his Spirit spoke to me that day through the words of that song.

I cannot promise that you will receive the same kind of direct revelation in your own journey. You might; you might not. What I can assure you of, however, is that in Christ, God's love is yours, no matter how little dignity you may feel.

Weakness is good?

Throughout his ministry, Jesus takes objection to the self-made and self-righteous, instead drawing to himself those who recognise their dependence on him.

It's too simple to say that those who have no money or power are the chosen ones of Christ. Rather, as we look at Jesus in the Gospels, what we see is his heart for the needy.

- Zacchaeus, with all his wealth, runs just to get a glimpse of Jesus in Luke 19.

- The Roman centurion acknowledges the limitations of his own authority in Luke 7.

- The bleeding woman just wants to touch the garments of Jesus in Mark 5.

- The paralysed man is lowered through the roof in Mark 2.

- The repentant criminal is remembered by Jesus on the cross in Luke 23.

When Jesus sees the need of people who realise their dependence on him, his heart overflows with mercy.

In John 5, Jesus arrives at a pool of healing, where different people gather, including the blind, the lame and the paralysed. John tells us of a man who has been an invalid for 38 years. We aren't told whether he has been coming to the pool for all that time, but it's fair to say this probably isn't his first visit. And yet, despite the belief that the pool holds healing properties, nobody stops to help this man.

Until Jesus arrives.

When Jesus saw him lying there and learned that he had been in this condition for a long time, he asked him, "Do you want to get well?"

> *"Sir," the invalid replied, "I have no one to help me into the pool when the water is stirred. While I am trying to get in, someone else goes down ahead of me."*
>
> *Then Jesus said to him, "Get up! Pick up your mat and walk." At once the man was cured; he picked up his mat and walked.* JOHN 5 v 6-9

When nobody else will help, Jesus does. And it isn't with water, but with words.

There is something about acute dependence that is considered unattractive in our self-made society. But in these times, when we appear to be in the most need, our dependence on Jesus is brought sharply into focus.

How brokenness can lead us to the truth

Of course, it's not as if we only need God when we're down and out. We need him every day. He puts breath in our lungs. Our hearts beat because he allows it. We can work in our jobs because he has provided the abilities and opportunities for us to do so. Our dependence never changes—it's just that in our sinful hearts it's easy to forget it. Sometimes, it takes a moment of brokenness to remember the truth.

This kind of brokenness is not specific to those of us with mental illness. It applies to all. Depression and anxiety do not in themselves make us faulty or unworthy. No, they are indicative of the deeper problem of a broken creation, which is the cause of all the hardship we experience in our lives. It is only because of Christ that this brokenness will one day come to an end.

You may live with mental illness for a while, or for the rest of your life. However, the extent to which this affects your daily life will fluctuate. When you are having a good day, praise God for this mercy. When you are having a bad day, know that God is still for you and not against you. His love never changes, and salvation is not dependent on our ability to function how we would like.

When we are down and out, in need of healing, the words Jesus brings us in his Spirit resound most loudly. We are loved by God, as seen most clearly in Christ's sacrificial death on the cross. This is our gospel identity—not that we are wealthy, successful, capable or esteemed. Our identity is that we are loved and accepted, and in our moments of deepest darkness, love and acceptance is what we crave. We just want to know that everything will be okay. It will be, even if relief in this life is not assured. That is why we can sing in all seasons that we have a reason to worship.

For reflection

Brokenness is not easy, but it can help you see more clearly your dependence on the love of God.

CHAPTER 3
FEELINGS

Pre-sermon jitters

I once heard that more people are afraid of public speaking than they are of death. Or, as Jerry Seinfeld put it, "Most people would prefer to be lying in the casket rather than giving the eulogy".

While I can understand this, I personally enjoy speaking to audiences. It's one of the reasons I went into ministry. And yet, for something that brings me such satisfaction, I still feel nervous in the lead-up to every sermon. I still like to do a mock run-through in front of the mirror the night before. And I still worry that I'll forget what I want to say, or make some unfortunate slip of the tongue.

God surprises me every time. Rarely do the words come out poorly, and even if they do, it seems that people are still encouraged by his word. You'd think it would be enough to stop me feeling nervous the next time around.

It isn't.

These feelings belie a truth that is unchanging. If God has blessed me with a gift, he will use that gift as he wishes. The feeling may be real to me, but it does not impact the reality of God's power.

The limitations of feelings

A good deal of psychological theory, particularly Cognitive Behaviour Therapy (CBT), encourages individuals to challenge their feelings. I have experienced this as a patient and found it to be very helpful. (See chapter 11 on page 91 for more on the various talking therapies.) Feelings often give rise to thoughts, and these are not always true. To use my own example, I *feel* nervous, and so I *think* I can't preach. Yet I know that God has gifted me to preach.

When it comes to mental illness, our feelings can be very misleading. I say this because a change in how we feel about God can be one of the main manifestations of depression or anxiety. This can be very distressing for a Christian, yet how we feel about God does **not** impact who he actually is.

- We may feel angry about our circumstances, which leads to the thought that God hates us. He doesn't.

- We may feel lonely, which leads to the thought that God has abandoned us. He hasn't.

- We may feel hopeless, which leads to the thought that there is nothing left to live for. There is.

If I haven't already made this clear, let me reinforce the point once more—**if you have given your life to Christ, your identity in the gospel does not change**. You are beloved by God and accepted by him in spite of all your flaws. But we sometimes find this impossible to *feel*.

In my case, my experience in the psychiatric hospital led to a clarification of my gospel identity. But this is not always the case, even for me.

The brokenness I experienced on the eve of my 30th birthday was not my first encounter with depression. It was the darkest, but not the first.

When I initially experienced depression in my early twenties, it was accompanied by deep spiritual dryness. Not only did I feel God was unloving, but I began to feel as though he may not even be real. For a Christian, this can be one of the most difficult challenges of mental illness—the lines between heart, soul and mind seem nearly impossible to separate. Yet in these moments, it is critical to remember that *feelings* are not necessarily *truths*.

Anxiety and depression can so easily convince us of lies. Our thoughts will go to all sorts of places—"I'm unworthy", "I will never amount to anything", "I am incapable", "This is going to fail", "This person doesn't care anymore". These thoughts can then lead to feelings of hopelessness, despondency and disillusionment.

These kinds of thoughts are not always true—in fact they rarely are—but it doesn't change the way we feel about them.

Has God deserted us? No. Can it feel as if he has? Absolutely. Your gospel identity tells you that you are loved. Your mind may tell you that you are unlovable.

Walking in the footsteps of others

The importance of understanding who we are before God is not new. The Psalms are common sources of comfort for those in times of trial, and for good reason. They speak candidly of the wrestle we face in this fallen world while at the same time resting in the goodness and sovereignty of God. Wrestle and rest—this is the normal experience of any Christian.

King David, in Psalm 13, speaks honestly about his plight. Yet the darkness he experiences does not have to exclude him from what he knows of the nature of God:

> *How long, LORD? Will you forget me for ever?*
> *How long will you hide your face from me?*
> *How long must I wrestle with my thoughts*
> *and day after day have sorrow in my heart?*

How long will my enemy triumph over me?

Look on me and answer, LORD my God.
Give light to my eyes, or I will sleep in death,
and my enemy will say, "I have overcome him,"
and my foes will rejoice when I fall.

But I trust in your unfailing love;
my heart rejoices in your salvation.
I will sing the LORD's praise,
for he has been good to me.

PSALM 13

King David's honesty is refreshing. He is open with God about what he thinks. He believes that God has forgotten him—that the Lord has hidden himself from him. This leads to feelings of sorrow, abandonment and grief.

Yet this is just how he *feels*, and nothing more. I do not want to pretend for one moment that feelings don't matter. I have felt the pain first-hand of deep darkness and thoughts that never seem to end. In the lead-up to my hospital stay, my feelings were in such a heightened state that they were unbearable.

But David doesn't just end with his feelings. He rests in what he *knows*.

He knows God has unfailing love for him, and that in his salvation he can rejoice, for the Lord has been good to him.

Is this not still true of us? In our depression, in our anxiety, we feel as though God is far away, or even non-existent. We question our place before him to the point of having doubts as to whether we have a Saviour at all.

We ask why he is not rescuing us from our darkness. These are questions we often have no answer for, and so we are left disillusioned.

But in these moments, the truths of God have not ceased. Just as David can rejoice in his salvation, so too can we take refuge in ours.

God is not dependent on us

In all seasons of life, the sacrifice of Christ shows that God has not spared even his own Son in his loving pursuit of us. This is why we need to hold on to the promises we have, because if we were to leave it to our feelings alone, the darkness would become a reality that has no hope. But to be a Christian is to have an undeniable hope.

Reflecting on your gospel identity—the fact that you are chosen and accepted by God because of Christ—enables you to find rest. When we doubt God's goodness, or even his existence, remembrance can be one of our most powerful allies. Just as David remembers his salvation in darkness, so too can we. We may never find out this side of heaven why we experience depression and anxiety, but this doesn't have to mean we have a God who does not care for us.

Romans 5 v 8 is a beautiful verse to remind us of this. Paul's letter to the church in Rome can often feel dense in theology and history, but in the midst of this are little nuggets of the simplest truths of who God is:

> *But God demonstrates his own love for us in this: while we were still sinners, Christ died for us.*
>
> ROMANS 5 v 8

Paul tells us in Romans 5 that we have peace with God because of what Christ has done for us. It is not because of who *we* are, but because of who *he* is. We are reminded that we don't need to be at war with him, and he is certainly not at war with us. We have a God who cares for us, who loves us—and we know this because he sent his Son while we were still far from him.

We would be wise to separate our feelings from what we know to be true of the gospel. We do not suppress and bottle up our feelings until we burst—that route is unhelpful. But in those times when we feel as if our spiritual health has suffered on account of our mental health, we choose to remember God's unfailing love— love that we can be sure of no matter how we may feel.

For reflection

Feelings don't always provide the clearest indicator of who God is and his love for us. Instead, take rest in the very core of the gospel message—that we know God loves us because he sent his Son for us while we were still far off.

CHAPTER 4
SIN

An expensive lesson learned

One of my proudest achievements is that I've never failed a driving exam. Until my mid-twenties, I'd also never had an accident. Growing up, my peers would fly around the local neighbourhoods. But my happy place was as a "grandpa" behind the wheel.

Despite my driving style, I don't mind music blaring while on the road. And it was one day, while AC/DC's "Thunderstruck" was thumping through the speakers, that my flawless driving record came to an end.

Having stopped at an intersection, I scanned for approaching cars. They had right of way and it was my job to wait. Finally, a break in the traffic emerged, except for one car whose driver was indicating that he was about to turn off.

I trusted his indicator, and drove out.

But he didn't turn, and instead of pulling into a side street, he ploughed into my driver's side door.

The driver refused to admit he had indicated, so the accident was deemed my fault. It was an error in judgment that cost me several thousand dollars.

Whose fault?

Who was at fault in the accident? Was it the driver, who drove straight on despite his indication? Or was it me, who trusted the indicator and failed to give right of way?

The question of blame is a deeply controversial aspect of any Christian discussion of mental illness. Who's to "blame" for anxiety and depression? Are they sinful? Could they possibly be our own fault? Or are we victims to chemical imbalances that are out of our control?

These are hard questions to answer, and some people may feel we shouldn't even be asking them.

This topic can be a mental-health minefield. Some Christians conclude that mental illness is purely a spiritual problem that needs to be addressed biblically and through prayer. Others see it entirely as an illness caused by a brain that is malfunctioning. And still others consider that it's probably a bit of both. So how do we negotiate this minefield?

How should Christians approach this question within a gospel worldview?

The general answer

The first conclusion we must make is that mental illness is a result of the sinful state of humanity. Ever since the fall in Genesis 3, when Adam and Eve rebelled against God for the first time, our world has been spoiled by sin (our rebellion against God). If the fall had not taken place, mental illness would not be in the world (neither would any illness). And so, depression and anxiety are certainly consequences of sin in the general sense.

This allows us to find genuine hope as we look forward to the return of Christ and the promised new creation (Revelation 21 v 1-4). We eagerly wait for a reality free of the consequences of sin, and which will therefore be free of mental illness. Romans 8 tells us that our mortal bodies and minds will one day be restored in the way in which they were always designed to function.

It can be easy to blame God for our depression and anxiety, but he is in fact the only one who offers a way out. While it's right to lament the effects of the fall over our lives, we also know that we await a greater day. And when we remember Christ on the cross, we can trust that God's heart is one of love. He is bringing everything together for his purposes, even though we don't always understand how.

The specific answer

And so, the general answer is fairly straightforward. Without the fall there would have been no pain. In this way, sin is absolutely a cause of our mental illness.

The controversy arises when we get more specific. Is there something the individual is doing that is leading to their depression or anxiety? To use my own story, was it my fault that I ended up in a psychiatric hospital? Did I make a series of poor choices? Was I unwilling to rest in the promises of God for my future direction?

Possibly.

When I was growing up, my dad had a sign on his desk which read, "Do not worry about tomorrow—God is already there" (see Matthew 6 and Luke 12). But in many ways, my actions communicated that God could *not* be trusted with my future, and that *I* had to be in control of every step.

Yet I can also see how I was susceptible to depression and anxiety from a young age. I was not depressed as a child, but I was always sensitive. I would get very distressed if I ever got into trouble with a teacher. I also remember idealistically dreaming of the future in a way which, in hindsight, was setting me up for disappointment and disillusionment.

Asking where our depression and anxiety came from can be helpful. We can start to identify root causes and therefore find ways to best move forward. For many of us this is a good thing to do, though I don't recommend trying it on your own. Instead, ask a friend for help. If possible, choose someone who knows you well enough to have insight into your life, and who loves you enough to tell you the truth. A friend like this is a gift from the Lord. They can help you to look at your own depression or anxiety carefully but safely.

Asking where our illness comes from can be helpful, but there is risk involved as well. Mentally replaying actions and choices can be like adding fuel to the fire. Our minds are already in overdrive, and we find it hard to switch off. The last thing we need is to be revisiting everything over and over, only to come to the conclusion that we are to blame.

The beauty of a gospel identity is that it allows us to be liberated from the bondage of our sin. This is true whether it be sin in the general or specific sense.

This means we don't have to go back and analyse every single mistake we ever made. Yes, there is wisdom in learning from the lessons of the past. And psychological theory teaches us to be aware of our early warning signs and to challenge unhealthy thoughts and actions. So if I begin to go down a road of dreaming of every career possible, I ought to remember the mistakes of my past. These can be helpful things to do, if they allow us to have a better understanding of who we are.

Critically, however, we do not need to *condemn* ourselves for the errors we make. Why? Because Christ does not condemn us either. Scripture is clear that we ought to live changed lives, but this is not sustained through self-condemnation, but out of gratitude for what Jesus has done.

> *Since, then, you have been raised with Christ, set your hearts on things above, where Christ is, seated at the right hand of God. Set your minds on things above, not on earthly things. For you died, and your life is now hidden with Christ in God. When Christ, who is your life, appears, then you also will appear with him in glory.*
>
> *Put to death, therefore, whatever belongs to your earthly nature...* COLOSSIANS 3 V 1-5

Two conclusions. One answer.

Let's say you conclude that your depression and anxiety are due to the generally fallen nature of the world: that is, you have been created with a biological propensity for anxiety and depression. What is the antidote for your problem? It is the reality that there will be a day when your body and mind will be made new. Your eternal reality is marked with no more crying and no more pain (Revelation 21 v 1-4). And this is made possible for you because of Jesus.

Alternatively, let's say you conclude that your depression or anxiety have resulted from a mismatch between the Bible's instructions and your decisions. You haven't trusted God or you have lived foolishly. What is the antidote to your problem? The forgiveness that is yours in Christ.

Jesus is the answer to both scenarios. He is always the solution to the problem of sin.

The gospel means that whatever the source of your mental illness, there is relief from the pain of condemnation and brokenness. God's plan for us is to live changed lives only through our gospel identity, which is beautifully summarised in Ephesians 2:

> *For it is by grace you have been saved, through faith— and this is not from yourselves, it is the gift of God— not by works, so that no one can boast. For we are God's handiwork, created in Christ Jesus to do good works, which God prepared in advance for us to do.*
>
> Ephesians 2 v 8-10

For reflection

Mental illness can be attributed to the general fallenness of creation, or specific transgressions of your own heart, or a combination of the two. Whatever the source, you can rest in the fact that there is relief in the gospel.

CHAPTER 5
HOPE

Hope is a powerful motivator. Hope of recovery sustains the patient with a life-threatening illness. Hope of graduation keeps the student hard-working. Hope of financial freedom enables the investor to put their own assets on the line.

Martin Luther reasoned that "everything that is done in this world is done by hope".[2]

Yet hope can prove to be an elusive trait for the depressive.

Ironically, I don't believe I became depressed because I felt hopeless. Instead, one of my triggers was an inflated sense of optimism. In putting my hope in the things of this world, the gap between fantasy and reality widened, and I became disillusioned with life itself.

It was misplaced hope that led me to hopelessness.

Disneyworld 2010

In January 2010, my wife, Lara, and I embarked on a gap year. In my Australian culture, it's almost a rite of passage that young adults will "find themselves" by travelling the world. We will explore as far as our dollars take us.

We took our gap year later than usual. Rather than go at the age of 18 with the desire to party until we could party no more, we were 25 and wanted to see the world together. I had very little experience of travelling, and so was extremely excited about this trip.

Four months into the year came a highly anticipated visit to Disneyworld. For the unfailing optimist, the "happiest place on earth" was sure to fulfil all my hopes and dreams. And in many ways, we had a great time. I particularly liked the waterslides!

But I also remember a distinct sense of shallowness about the whole experience. People seemed far from happy. Children complained about how much walking they had to do. Adults complained about the price of food. The heat was sapping. Happiness was manufactured and my hope had proved to be misplaced. I was disillusioned.

It was during a night back at the hotel that I realised for the first time that something was seriously wrong with my mental state. I remember lying on the bed and having a complete attack of anxiety. I was so looking forward to this time together, and it just felt futile. The pursuit of fun was nothing but just that—a pursuit. The desire to have the time of my life had disappointed me. It was never going to live up to the perfection I had imagined. In that moment I felt as though life was just one big let-down. If what I had been looking for couldn't even be found at Disneyworld, what hope was there?

For those of you who haven't experienced depression, this may seem astonishing, but it was on that night that the first suicidal thought entered my head.

Even better than a wedding

Since that time, it has been one of my greatest honours to be asked to preach at the wedding of two of my friends. When I asked which passage they wanted, they surprised me by choosing Revelation 21:

> Then I saw "a new heaven and a new earth," for the first heaven and the first earth had passed away, and there was no longer any sea. I saw the Holy City, the new Jerusalem, coming down out of heaven from God, prepared as a bride beautifully dressed for her husband. And I heard a loud voice from the throne saying, "Look! God's dwelling place is now among the people, and he will dwell with them. They will be his people, and God himself will be with them and be their God. 'He will wipe every tear from their eyes. There will be no more death' or mourning or crying or pain, for the old order of things has passed away."

> *He who was seated on the throne said, "I am making*
> *everything new!" Then he said, "Write this down, for*
> *these words are trustworthy and true."*
>
> *He said to me: "It is done. I am the Alpha and the*
> *Omega, the Beginning and the End. To the thirsty I*
> *will give water without cost from the spring of the water*
> *of life. Those who are victorious will inherit all this,*
> *and I will be their God and they will be my children.*
>
> REVELATION 21 V 1-7

I asked why they had chosen this passage. They told me that although this day, their wedding day, was a most momentous occasion, they knew a day was coming that would be even greater.

Here was a couple living with a real hope: a living hope. Theirs was not a fatalistic view that this world has nothing good to offer. Their wedding day was joyous. It was right for us to celebrate. But they also recognised that complete hope is only found in the new creation. This is not a maturity that I had at their age.

Hope that does not shame

Depression can turn life into the darkest of pits. Nothing seems to taste sweet or smell fragrant. Worse still, we can easily feel as though everything will remain this way forever. But our gospel identity reminds us that because of Jesus, our permanent reality is one where there is no more crying or pain.

This does not mean we just give up on this life. God has given us his creation to tend to and live in—to worship him with each day of life that he grants us. Yet if we put our complete and final hope in this fractured world, we set ourselves up for inevitable disappointment. Being a Christian and being a perfectionist are ultimately incompatible. The perfection we need comes only from Christ—never from our own achievements.

The beauty of the gospel is this—while our disappointments and failures can evaporate our sense of misplaced hope, the love of Jesus means there is a hope far better than anything else.

> *¹Therefore, since we have been justified through faith, we have peace with God through our Lord Jesus Christ, ²through whom we have gained access by faith into this grace in which we now stand. And we boast in the hope of the glory of God. ³Not only so, but we also glory in our sufferings, because we know that suffering produces perseverance; ⁴perseverance, character; and character, hope. ⁵And* **hope does not put us to shame***, because God's love has been poured out into our hearts through the Holy Spirit, who has been given to us.*
>
> ROMANS 5 v 1-5 (*bold text mine*)

Because of the salvation that is ours through faith, we now have peace and hope that no other source can provide. Verse 5 presents a solution that Disneyworld could never offer. And notice what Paul says in verse 3—we are able to "glory in our sufferings". Why? Because we have a hope that is given to us through the Holy Spirit, and this is hope *that does not put us to shame.*

"And" or "but"

Inherent in this idea is a concept that a psychologist friend first introduced me to—dialectic behaviour. In my understanding, this is the claim that two seemingly contradictory notions can both be true at the same time. This hinges on a small but powerful use of language.

I wonder if you have ever considered the power of the words "but" or "and". If you're like me, probably never.

But consider the implications if I say, "The gospel provides hope *but* I feel hopeless".

The use of the word "but" serves to negate the first part of the sentence. In other words, my sense of hopelessness wins out over the hope that the gospel provides.

Now, what if I say, "The gospel provides hope *and* I feel hopeless"?

This changes things. Now I can feel hopeless *and* the hope of the gospel can still be true. The sun can be shining *and* I can feel low. My lowness does not stop the sun from shining. In the same way, the hopelessness we can feel does not have the power to stop the hope we have. God is bigger than that.

Better than our wildest dreams

If Martin Luther is correct, and everything we do is done by hope, then we press on in worship of the Lord. This can be hard for anyone, and mental illness adds another layer of complexity because of how we feel. We must remember, however, that heaven will be no Disneyworld experience. Everything we are waiting for will come to be, and even more than we could imagine. In the midst of darkness and how we feel, the truth of what we know in the Lord inspires us to press on.

I was a fool for thinking that my Disneyworld experience would be perfect. I am not a fool for thinking that my eternal reality will be perfect. For that reason I will not be put to shame. We have peace with the Father through the Son, which is a hope that has been put on our hearts by the Holy Spirit. We have a great God.

We wait for God's perfect timing

I will mention this in greater detail in chapter 9 (page 75), but for now let me say that finding rest in this hope does not give us a licence for suicide.

Let me assure you that I do empathise with how you may feel. You may feel desperate to leave this world and be with the Lord. But escaping the pain and disappointment of this world for the hope that is to come is not what Paul is getting at here. Notice again how he says that the peace we have with God enables us to endure suffering, because we know of the glory that is to come. Paul does not say that suffering is easy—but he does say that it is *possible* to endure because of our gospel identity.

Paul's suffering was a physical persecution. Ours is a mental trauma. The approach, however, remains the same. Press on. And if you're at a point where you're contemplating suicide, seek help immediately. *Right now.**

Heaven is not a reason to take our own lives. Life is a gift from God and your identity in Christ means that you can navigate through it with purpose.

For reflection

We live in light of the hope we have, and this enables us to endure suffering—bringing worship to God in all seasons.

*If you are feeling desperate right now, please contact a pastor, counsellor, doctor or trusted Christian friend. Or see page 137 at the back of this book for a list of helplines and resources.

CHAPTER 6
ATTACK

"The Rumble in the Jungle"

In October 1974, perhaps the most famous boxing match ever took place. It was known as "The Rumble in the Jungle". Muhammad Ali and George Foreman fought in Kinshasa, in what was then known as Zaire (now the Democratic Republic of the Congo).

As they arrived in Africa, Ali was immediately touted as the good guy. The Congolese would cry out in the weeks leading up to the fight, "Ali, boma ye", which literally translated as "Ali, kill him".

But Ali was a massive underdog. Foreman was a giant, and it was believed that Ali was past his prime.

Yet despite the odds, Ali weathered a barrage of punches from the first to the 8th round. With a few seconds left in the 8th round, he landed the knockout blow—a right hook to the head. Foreman staggered, and he began to fall. As far as the outcome was concerned, it was over. As Foreman staggered, Ali was in a position to throw one more punch.

And he didn't.

He just watched his opponent fall, fist clenched but never to throw his arm out. The fight was already over.

Spiritual attack

Like all analogies, this has limitations, but it does serve to illustrate an important truth of the gospel. On the cross, Jesus Christ delivered the knockout blow to Satan. By his perfect sacrifice, Jesus has defeated sin, death and the devil himself. The cross confirmed what we always knew—that God is stronger than evil. At the moment, the world still turns in its brokenness, and so in one sense Satan is still in the fight, but the result is inevitable.

Acknowledging the work of Satan is a difficult line to tread. On the one hand, it can be tempting to dismiss his power, or even existence, altogether. In a modern world that is reluctant to believe in the supernatural, a wrestle between good and evil can seem archaic. On the other hand, we can attribute too much power to Satan, as if he can prevent the plans of God.

Both of these perspectives are flawed. In reality, while Christians must acknowledge that Satan is both real and powerful, we face this battle with the God who is infinitely more powerful. The Lord always wins.

The apostle Paul treads this line in his letter to the Ephesians:

> *Finally, be strong in the Lord and in his mighty power. Put on the full armour of God, so that you can take your stand against the devil's schemes. For our struggle is not against flesh and blood, but against the rulers, against the authorities, against the powers of this dark world and against the spiritual forces of evil in the heavenly realms. Therefore put on the full armour of God, so that when the day of evil comes, you may be able to stand your ground, and after you have done everything, to stand.* EPHESIANS 6 V 10-13

The lies of mental illness

In my experience, one of the most difficult things when dealing with the pain of mental illness is that our mental and spiritual health are so often inseparable.

In chapter 2, I mentioned that while I lay on the floor in the psychiatric hospital, I was able to sing the words of a song which reminded me of God's unfailing love in all seasons. But this was not always the case. After Disneyworld, I remember going through a time of deep, spiritual darkness where I wondered if God was a constructed figment of my imagination. Such was the darkness and pain of how I felt. Everything I had ever put my trust in was suddenly in flux.

As a Christian, I think this is truly one of the greatest tragedies of mental illness. The very nature of depression and anxiety are that they tell us lies about what is real, and what is not. In my own case, mental illness has told me lies such as these:

- My life is never going to amount to anything.
- I've got nothing to be thankful for.
- I don't know if God is even there.
- I'm always going to feel this way.
- I am unloveable.

I know these are lies because they contradict the truths of God's word. Maybe you can relate to some of these, or perhaps in your own mental illness you have told yourself others. But at its core, the very nature of mental illness is a failure of the brain to remain balanced in its function. This is the case whether you live with anxiety, depression or any other brokenness of the brain.

But as Christians, we need to remember that our battle is not just in the mental realm, but the spiritual also. A literal translation of "Satan" can be "the accuser", or "the adversary". Put simply, Satan sees his job as robbing us of the truth that we know we have as children of God. He strives to deceive us, as he did in Eden. If we consider the serpent's words in the Genesis account of creation, we learn much of our enemy's strategies.

Did God really say?

The haunting words which the devil speaks to Eve still resound and give an insight into how our enemy prowls.

> **Did God really say**, *"You must not eat from any tree in the garden"?* Genesis 3 v 1 *(bold text mine)*

The answer to Satan's question is painfully clear. God laid out the truth in brutal simplicity just one chapter earlier.

> *... but you must not eat from the tree of the knowledge of good and evil, for when you eat from it you will certainly die.* Genesis 2 v 17

Satan's words are an outright lie, designed to take Adam and Eve away from what God has proclaimed as truth.

And when we fast forward to the New Testament, we see a re-enactment of sorts when Satan tries to tempt Jesus. This time, however, his deceptive attempts fail.

In Luke 4, we see Satan try to lure Jesus away from the Father. Verse 2 describes our Saviour as hungry, and so the enemy tries to make Jesus fall away from righteousness three times when he is at his weakest.

And when Satan fails, he leaves, but not before Luke gives us a critical insight into how the adversary operates:

> *When the devil had finished all this tempting, he left him until **an opportune time**.*
>
> LUKE 4 V 13 *(bold text mine)*

Opportunistic.

This is how Satan works. He saw an opportunity in the garden to lure Adam and Eve from the truth. It worked. He saw an opportunity in the wilderness to lure away Jesus. It didn't.

For the Christian enduring mental illness, Satan will undoubtedly see this as an opportunity to spread the kinds of lies that he revels in. When did Satan attack Jesus? When he was weak, tired, hungry and alone. And so, when we too are weak, Satan attempts to pounce. Let us not forget that sobering reality.

If a translation of Satan is "accuser", how is it that a perennial liar accuses? He does so by attempting to rob us of our gospel truth. Paul tells us in Romans 8 that "there is now no condemnation for those who are in Christ Jesus" (v 1). Satan may try and make us feel guilty or unloved, but these feelings do not and will not ever rob us of the reality of Christ's victory. On the cross, with three simple words, Jesus declared the truth about our battle with sin and condemnation (John 19 v 30): *It is finished.*

The accuser continues to ask the question "Did God really say?" that we first heard him utter in Eden.

As Christians, we know we can confidently claim that we are beloved children of God, redeemed by the blood of Christ and victorious in his resurrection. But Satan continues to try to convince us that this is not true—that we are not redeemed, but rather, under condemnation.

What better time to attempt this than when our mental states are at their most fragile? I have little doubt that we experience spiritual attack through mental illness. Why wouldn't Satan want to tempt us to fail to trust in the promises of God in our darkest hour?

- "Did God really say that you could trust him with your future?"

- "Did God really say that you were accepted by him?"

- "Did God really say that nothing could separate you from his love?"

Victory is yours

Satan will use any means possible, and depression and anxiety are an easy way in. But at our lowest, we must remember the great truth of our gospel identity—that we have One who is truly victorious.

True victory comes in the gospel of Christ. Satan knew he was in trouble when Jesus couldn't be tempted in the wilderness. This wasn't just another Adam—this was the One whom Adam could not be. It was a defeat that Satan first tasted at the beginning of Jesus' ministry, and it was a defeat that culminated on the cross. Through Jesus, humans can be reconciled to God in a relationship that Satan is unable to break, as much as he tries.

Though anxiety and depression tell you lies, you can trust in the words of victory that the gospel brings. If your mental and spiritual health feel inseparable, run to the words of Scripture. Revelation 20 and 21 tell us of the victory that we have in Christ, and no attempt of Satan to rob God's people of their glory can succeed.

Attack is Satan's game; victory is not.

> *When the thousand years are over, Satan will be released from his prison and will go out to deceive the nations in the four corners of the earth—Gog and Magog—and to gather them for battle. In number they are like the sand on the seashore. They marched across the breadth of the earth and surrounded the camp of God's people, the city he loves. But fire came down from heaven and devoured them. And the devil, who deceived them, was thrown into the lake of burning sulphur, where the beast and the false prophet had been thrown. They will be tormented day and night for ever and ever.* REVELATION 20 V 7-10

The role of the 1000 years has been long debated, and it is not the purpose of this book to continue that debate. Whatever one's exact understanding of this text, one thing is for sure. When Satan thinks he is about to devour the people of God, *he will be devoured himself.* It is an image of dramatic irony. And notice what John says Satan's task is—twice in this passage John calls him the one who deceives.

But it is Satan who is deceived, for who is he to rob God of his glory? No, if anxiety or depression ever darken your gaze on the brilliance of Jesus, remember the words of Revelation 20, and bask in the glory of Revelation 21:

> *I did not see a temple in the city, because the Lord God Almighty and the Lamb are its temple. The city does not need the sun or the moon to shine on it, for the glory of God gives it light, and the Lamb is its lamp. The nations will walk by its light, and the kings of the earth will bring their splendour into it. On no day will its gates ever be shut, for there will be no night there. The glory and honour of the nations will be brought into it. Nothing impure will ever enter it, nor will anyone who does what is shameful or deceitful, but only those whose names are written in the Lamb's book of life.* REVELATION 21 V 22-27

The victory that comes with your gospel identity changes everything. This victory means that your righteousness is not dependent on your state of mental health. Though you may be in the pit of despair, take rest in the true words of Revelation. And though you may have fears about your future, or pain in your past, remember what your ultimate, eternal reality holds for you.

Satan will prowl and try to deceive, but nothing can remove the truth of the promises of God. The deceiver may, and probably will, use mental illness as a way to bring down your perceived spiritual reality. Yet we must remember that our identity is found in the death and resurrection of the One who could not be deceived, even at his weakest.

For reflection

Satan will tempt and try to deceive, but know that victory is yours in Christ. Pray against his attack, and that you will see the light of the Lamb in the darkest of times. Satan will wage war against all of us, and so let us not give up praying for others who are burdened.

CHAPTER 7
MEANING

An incisive question

In 2011 I saw a psychologist for the first time. I found it such a relief to talk through some of the issues that had been consuming my mental energy for so long.

Years have passed since those first sessions, but there is still one moment which is emblazoned on my consciousness. As well as providing words of comfort, this Christian brother also challenged me in my thought patterns.

I explained to him that first situation at Disneyworld (see page 42), and how I had become increasingly jaded. I told him that life was not turning out as I had always dreamed. I had grand visions for the future, and when I realised that not all were going to come to fruition, my world was shattered.

This was a radical departure from the "you can achieve anything" message that society had fed me from a young age. I had bought into it, and was hooked on the notion. If I put in enough effort, anything was possible. The problem was, I didn't just want to achieve anything; I wanted to achieve *everything*. I wanted to be wealthy; I wanted to be successful; I wanted to be a good family man; I wanted to be a leader and have great influence; I wanted spare time. I wanted it all, and I believed that if I strategised hard enough, I could have it.

As I explained my mental journey to the psychologist, he said something that stopped me in my tracks:

"Chris, it sounds like you want happiness to be the goal of your life."

I thought about his statement for a moment.

I knew he was right—and even worse, I knew where he was going with his line of thought. I was tempted to resist the notion, but swallowed my pride and told him he was correct.

Then came the question:

"Have you considered that God might want the goal of your life not to be happiness, but maturity?"

The question floored me because I had never considered it before. I knew life wasn't working; but I didn't know why. It hadn't occurred to me that my life goal may not be the Lord's.

What's it all about?

Why are we here? Do we exist to reach self-fulfilment, or are we here to grow into the realisation that our true identity is in Christ? What if life isn't meant to ultimately be about happiness?

When we look to Jesus, we do not see a man striving for happiness. In one of the greatest displays of his humanity, we see Christ's brutally honest and intimate prayer at Gethsemane. He is about to be crucified, and he knows it.

> *Then Jesus went with his disciples to a place called Gethsemane, and he said to them, "Sit here while I go over there and pray." He took Peter and the two sons of Zebedee along with him, and he began to be sorrowful and troubled. Then he said to them, "My soul is overwhelmed with sorrow to the point of death. Stay here and keep watch with me."*
>
> *Going a little farther, he fell with his face to the ground and prayed, "My Father, if it is possible, may this cup be taken from me. **Yet not as I will, but as you will."***
>
> MATTHEW 26 v 36-39 *(bold text mine)*

Not as I will, but as you will. Here is maturity. In this one act, Jesus is the greatest example of loving God and loving his neighbour.

Jesus had every right to claim what was his: comfort, success, esteem and prestige. He was God on earth. But he didn't. Rather, he is maturity personified—the Son of God is so in tune with the will of the Father that he can lay everything aside for us.

As the apostle Peter writes his first letter, happiness is not what he seeks for his readers either. Instead, he prepares them for suffering, insults and persecution:

> [12]*Dear friends, do not be surprised at the fiery ordeal that has come on you to test you, as though something strange were happening to you.* [13]*But rejoice inasmuch as you participate in the sufferings of Christ, so that you may be overjoyed when his glory is revealed.* [14]*If you are insulted because of the name of Christ, you are blessed, for the Spirit of glory and of God rests on you.* [15]*If you suffer, it should not be as a murderer or thief or any other kind of criminal, or even as a meddler.* [16]*However, if you suffer as a Christian, do not be ashamed, but praise God that you bear that name.*
>
> 1 PETER 4 V 12-16

Happiness or joy?

Whether it be external persecution or inner turmoil, the Christian life means participating in the sufferings of Christ (1 Peter 4 v 13). Happiness is not promised, but joy is. How? Because our identity in the Lord does not change on account of mood, or circumstance. For the depressive, this is a key concept to remember.

When we are happy, we can thank God for that. But when we are not happy, as is often the case when we are depressed or anxious, we are not left at a loss. Our life is not defined by this single emotion. Rather, our call is to maturity—to worship God in all seasons for who he is and what he has done.

> *Consider it pure joy, my brothers and sisters, whenever you face trials of many kinds, because you know that the testing of your faith produces perseverance. Let perseverance finish its work so that you may be mature and complete, not lacking anything. If any of you lacks wisdom, you should ask God, who gives generously to all without finding fault, and it will be given to you.*
>
> JAMES 1 V 2-5

Pursuing maturity, rather than happiness, has changed the way I think about my life. It allows me room to fail. It allows me room to be disappointed. It allows me room to find life hard. And most importantly, it allows me room to find joy in the midst of all seasons. I hope it will do the same for you.

Everything's not lost

One of my favourite songs of all time is "Everything's Not Lost" by Coldplay. The title itself gives me comfort and hope.

As Christians, we can confidently claim that in mental illness everything's not lost. As we've seen, Scripture shows us that we are to be more concerned with godly maturity than with happiness, and encourages us that hardship will produce good fruit. Depression and anxiety can increase our reliance on God's strength. A pursuit of holy living in the face of adversity is never a wasted experience.

If we loosen our grip on the pursuit of happiness, we can more readily deal with our anxiety and depression. The dark times we endure cannot destroy our identity in Christ. The relief this brings can ironically allow us to enjoy our lives all the more.

Let's remember that there are many gifts that the Lord has given us to delight in: the food we eat, the jobs we do, the families we love, the friends we enjoy. Give thanks to him for these blessings. But if our end goal is self-created happiness, even if based on things given to us by God, we will risk being destroyed by the anxiety and depression we wage war against on a daily basis. Instead, let's ask the Lord to help us make our goal a steadfast reliance on Christ, and ask him to use this to grow godly fruit in our lives.

For reflection

Are you pursuing happiness as your ultimate goal in life? In what ways does this show itself in your life? How can anxiety and depression clarify the call to follow Christ in joyful obedience?

CHAPTER 8
IDOLS

Winning the trophy

I love basketball. For eight months of the year, I invest time, thought and energy into following the sport I love.

Each July, the Finals of the NBA (US basketball league) arrive. This is the culmination of the hopes and dreams of players, coaches and executives. Everyone wants to be there, and yet only two of the thirty teams will make it.

As a fan, this is what I have waited for as well. Hours spent in watching games reach their climax in this month.

But July always ends.

One team wins. They are presented with a trophy and parade through the street of their hometown. Then what happens? Not satisfied with their achievements, the athletes go back and try to do it all over again. They may have a couple of weeks off, but then it's straight back into training.

For 29 of the teams, the year has ended in disappointment. For one team, it has ended in success, but even that single year's achievements aren't enough. There is the pressure to repeat.

The trophy has been idolised from afar for a year. And when it's gained, it doesn't prove ultimately satisfying.

Idol worship

We can't help but worship. As Christians, we believe that if we worship anything other than God himself, we set ourselves up for disappointment. At best, we may experience temporary satisfaction, but it never lasts. Our idol may not be a sporting trophy. It could be the "perfect" relationship, which proves to be imperfect. The dream job, which turns out to be less than a dream. These things fail to satisfy because it's only God who will never disappoint—his love is unconditional and our eternal reality will be flawless.

At all stages of life, whatever our age or circumstances, it's important that we bring our hearts before the Lord. It's right to regularly question our motives, and to ask ourselves what it is we are actually worshipping. This is true for all of us. However, we who wrestle with mental illness must also remember to be gracious to ourselves, for we have a Lord who is wonderfully gracious with us. We may find that in our darkest moments, worship simply looks like getting through each day that God has given us.

Let me say at this point that if you are in the midst of the darkest depression or most heightened anxiety, this may well be a chapter for another time. If so, it's fine to jump to chapter 9. *Really*.

But if you are in a season of recovery, I encourage you to bring your heart with humility before our gracious Lord.

Specific triggers

In order to establish how idolatry can play into mental illness, it's important for us to consider our specific triggers.

For example, why was it that I had my first suicidal thought at Disneyworld and not at home? Because I had put my complete hope in that experience, and it had left me disillusioned. I had come to idolise happiness, and I wasn't happy. It almost destroyed me.

Why did a decision about career lead to my admission to a psychiatric hospital? Why didn't it happen when I had to make a decision about which car to buy? Because I had come to put my hope and identity in what I did for work, and not in the car I drove.

You may consider yourself to be an "anxious person", or a "depressed person". This may be true, but it's important to go one step further in self-analysis. What are the triggers that get you down the most? What makes you the most anxious?

What is it that you dream about, but which, like the sporting trophy, never quite seems to satisfy you?

History repeats

In the Old Testament, idols primarily took the form of physical objects—false gods made of wood, stone and metal. They were an indication that God's people were not satisfied with his presence, and that they believed another deity could do what God could not.

We see this early in Israel's history at Mount Sinai. Moses has gone up the mountain to be with God. He receives the Ten Commandments. But the nation begins to grow restless. They become impatient while waiting for God to reveal himself, and so they take matters into their own hands:

> When the people saw that Moses was so long in coming down from the mountain, they gathered around Aaron and said, "Come, make us gods who will go before us. As for this fellow Moses who brought us up out of Egypt, we don't know what has happened to him."
>
> EXODUS 32 V 1-2

When we decide that God cannot be trusted, or is not sufficient for what we need, we choose to worship something else that we believe can be relied on more than him.

The New Testament shows us that *our* hearts are no different from those of the Israelites. Romans 1 tells us that people still replace God in all his majesty with things that do not come close in comparison.

Paul explains that the goodness and sufficiency of God have been made clear to all, but that our thoughts and hearts are easily swayed.

> *For since the creation of the world God's invisible qualities—his eternal power and divine nature—have been clearly seen, being understood from what has been made, so that people are without excuse.*
>
> *For although they knew God, they neither glorified him as God nor gave thanks to him, but their thinking became futile and their foolish hearts were darkened. Although they claimed to be wise, they became fools and exchanged the glory of the immortal God for images made to look like a mortal human being and birds and animals and reptiles.*   ROMANS 1 V 20-23

Idolatry and mental illness

Examining the influence of idolatry on our mental state is another controversial topic the Christian must wrestle with.

As we saw in the chapter on sin (page 33), we must not ignore the chemical and biological factors that can lead to depression and anxiety. I myself take medication (more on this later) to help with this balance, and it has been a significant blessing to me.

But I also know there have been times when I have not been satisfied with the goodness and provision of God, and this has triggered my depression and anxiety. Rarely is it an either/or equation—which means there is room for reflecting on our own hearts.

Rather than wishing away your depression and anxiety, it can be more helpful to reflect on the circumstances and instances that bring out your symptoms.

Do your unrealised career aspirations get you down? Have your kids not quite turned out the way you wanted? Is there never enough money to buy the things you want? Can your friends never do enough to support you? What causes you the most disappointment, frustration or disillusionment?

What do you think about when you are at your lowest or most anxious? In these moments you may just be able to identify an idol. And in this identification is the hope of breaking their stronghold.

This process takes a great deal of humility, and can often be nurtured in ongoing conversations with a caring and trusted friend. Asking somebody to speak into your life can bring insight into your own behaviours, beliefs and tendencies. Try and think of somebody who will not just identify an idol, but will have the love to walk with you through the process of healing and redemption from that idol's power.

Having a trusted Christian friend or pastor to share these things with is a great gift from the Lord. If you can't think of anyone, ask the Lord to show you someone who can help. It may be someone you never considered, but who turns out to be God's gift to you in your struggle.

Not ashamed to call me brother or sister

Breaking an idol is not just about turning away from what we do not like. It's about seeing the total supremacy of Christ over the idol. It's not enough for me to say, "Stop dreaming about career". Rather, I must conclude that who I am in Christ is better than any identity a career can give me.

But we do see Jesus, who was made lower than the angels for a little while, now crowned with glory and honour because he suffered death, so that by the grace of God he might taste death for everyone.

In bringing many sons and daughters to glory, it was fitting that God, for whom and through whom everything exists, should make the pioneer of their salvation perfect through what he suffered. Both the one who makes people holy and those who are made

> *holy are of the same family. So Jesus is not ashamed to*
> *call them brothers and sisters.* HEBREWS 2 V 9-11

Hebrews 2 tells us that Jesus became human in order to suffer death as our Saviour. And, as a human, Christ is not ashamed to call you and me brother or sister. Isn't that wonderful? The author of Hebrews also tells us that Jesus tasted death for everyone so that he would bring us to glory. A truth such as this allows me to see that even if I don't achieve everything I want to in this life, it doesn't destroy me. Even if I were the CEO of a Fortune 500 company, it would still be nothing in comparison with the treasured prize that awaits me. I am now Christ's brother and this is an identity that is better than any other.

This is what I realised in hospital the hard way. I didn't know what to do as a career, but I still had dignity because God loved me irrespective of my ability.

We don't examine the idols of our hearts so as to beat ourselves up. Our gospel identity tells us that we are wholly acceptable to God because of what *Jesus* has done. But if we want to live God-honouring lives in response to this great truth, it is right for us to reflect on how we sometimes seek to replace the glory of God with other things that cannot even compare.

Our gospel identity tells us that Jesus is everything we could have ever dreamed of—the forgiveness, love and hope that we have in him satisfy those internal cravings by which we are so often led astray. And when we do succumb to them, we can find refuge in God's mercy because of what Christ has done.

It could be that your depression and anxiety reveal something about the ways in which you become dissatisfied with God. If so, your gospel identity tells you that you can bring your heart to him with honesty, and rest in the grace that he has shown you in Christ.

For reflection

What are the main catalysts that spark your depression and anxiety? It could be work, money, comfort, happiness, family, friends etc. Bring these things to the Lord, ask for wisdom in seeing them for what they are, and pray that the Holy Spirit would remind you of the peace that comes from knowing Christ.

CHAPTER 9
SUICIDE

Note: *Did you jump straight to this chapter? If so, it will help you to know that the gospel identity I talk about here is unpacked in chapters 1 and 2. And if suicide is a worry for you right now, whether for yourself or someone else, please turn to page 137 to find where you can turn for help.*

The elephant in the room

I learned a great deal about other people and the effects of mental illness during my time in hospital. Everyone is there because they, or someone they know, have acknowledged that something is wrong. For me, it was my first admission to hospital. Others had been there on numerous occasions.

To one degree or another, we were all familiar with the process. During group therapy, we were encouraged to talk with honesty about our journeys. Yet even still, there was one topic that seemed taboo: suicide.

During one session, I remember the facilitator writing on the board the following words:

Mental illness: signs and symptoms

We were asked to share from our own experiences how we knew there may be a problem. Responses varied—weight loss or gain, changes in energy levels, inability to work, lack of enjoyment of life.

In my mind, I wanted to say "suicidal thoughts" but it didn't seem that anybody else wanted to talk about that. Eventually, the psychologist wrote it on the board herself. I don't assume that mental illness automatically leads to thoughts of suicide, but I have no doubt that some in the room were also thinking it but couldn't bring themselves to say it.

If there was ever an environment where the stigma of mental illness could be broken down, this would be it. And yet we still didn't want to talk about suicide.

Caught between two worlds

Christians face a unique tension when it comes to this life here on earth, because we believe there is a better life to come. We have the hope of an eternal reality, where there will be no more crying and no more pain (Revelation 21 v 4). We believe this is not an abstract dream, but that in Christ's death and resurrection it is our permanent home—a place where we do not have to endure the pain that comes with living in a fallen creation.

But this raises a tension. How do we have hope of the new creation without being *more* suicidal (because we long for what comes after death) than before? If we are struggling so much with depression and anxiety—if life is so very hard—does heaven give us an "out"?

Life and death

Philippians 1 is a key passage in our understanding of this issue. Rather than simply saying that suicide is not what God wants from us, the words of Paul also help us understand why.

> *For to me, to live is Christ and to die is gain.*
>
> PHILIPPIANS 1 V 21

When I was growing up, my youth leader at church had a tattoo which said, "To live is Christ", and his best friend had another tattoo which said, "To die is gain". These words were deeply confronting to me. At the time, in late high school, I could never imagine saying that dying was gain. Looking back, I think this was because I had not experienced enough suffering to see that the world in its present form was so broken.

How is it that, as Christians, we can say that dying is gain without falling into the trap of suicide? The answer is in the first part of the verse. Paul can value his life, even though dying is gain, because to live *is Christ*. While heaven is a gain in Paul's eyes, he isn't without purpose in the time God has given him here.

At this point in his ministry, he finds himself in chains for the gospel (Philippians 1 v 13) and yet even in his present circumstance, he understands that this is where God has placed him.

And because of my chains, most of the brothers and sisters have become confident in the Lord and dare all the more to proclaim the gospel without fear.

PHILIPPIANS 1 V 14

Yet, in his refreshing honesty, Paul still wrestles with whether he can go on for this purpose.

If I am to go on living in the body, this will mean fruitful labour for me. Yet what shall I choose? I do not know! I am torn between the two: I desire to depart and be with Christ, which is better by far; but it is more necessary for you that I remain in the body.

PHILIPPIANS 1 V 22-24

Paul understands that death will be a gain for him. He knows it is better, yet he presses on because there is much work left to do in his ministry.

You may be thinking that, unlike Paul, you don't have a ministry or call on your life, and therefore there isn't much keeping you here. Maybe mental illness has robbed you of the ability to function at a level that you would want to. That is hard to live with. But no matter who we are, the call God places on our life is the same as he placed on Paul's. Our life is Christ's, and he is our life, in all situations.

In some ways, depression and anxiety allow us to worship God more deeply. Why? Because it's harder to acknowledge that our life is still in Christ in these times. Yet if we are able in the midst of suffering to still call Jesus our Lord, we see just how deeply God's Spirit is at work within us, and we can thank him for that.

Pressing on

Paul's understanding of a gospel identity is not conditional on how he feels, or where he finds himself. Rather, the hope he has in Christ allows him to press on in all seasons. Honouring God in the face of suffering can be one of the most powerful testimonies to God's power. It may not look impressive, but the act of not succumbing to suicidal thoughts is in itself a reliance on God's strength. We eagerly anticipate the hope that we have, but we remember that God has created us for a common purpose—to honour and worship him with each day he gives us.

Unconditional

A fellow student at Bible college once told me that she did not believe those who commit suicide can be saved. I disagree. The moment we start placing conditions on God's grace is the moment we fail to understand grace. Please hear this—I do not believe suicide is honouring to God. It is a sin to end the life he has given you by your own hands. Yet, as with all sins, the blood of Jesus is powerful enough to cover it. Suicide is not an unforgivable sin, nor a sign that someone is not a Christian. But if you are a follower of Christ, please see that taking your life isn't what God would want. He has created you and made you to worship him with every breath of life he gives you.

If you are reading this, and have experienced the heart-wrenching loss of the death of a loved one to suicide, please know that there is grace for them if they were in Christ. I don't pretend that this takes away the pain, but there is comfort in God's mercy.

Paul yearns for the day when there will be no more suffering and no more pain, but until that day he knows that he is here for a purpose—and that is to honour and trust God with each day that he has been given. Grace has transformed him, the gospel has penetrated his heart, and he lives with this purpose through afflictions and trials.

> *Rejoice in the Lord always. I will say it again: rejoice! Let your gentleness be evident to all. The Lord is near. Do not be anxious about anything, but in every situation, by prayer and petition, with thanksgiving, present your requests to God. And the peace of God, which transcends all understanding, will guard your hearts and your minds in Christ Jesus.*
>
> PHILIPPIANS 4 v 4-7

For reflection

To live is Christ and to die is gain. These are both true, which means that no matter how dark life gets, we have a reason to press on in this life with our eyes still fixed on the new creation.

CHAPTER 10
HEALING

Swimming with whales

In the summer of 2012, my father-in-law Brian visited the remote Pacific nation of Tonga. The trip was the fulfilment of a dream he had to swim with whales.

It started as a typical holiday, with daily sunshine and relaxation. But it was his adventure beyond the reef that he was most looking forward to.

When the day arrived, it took about three hours to journey into deep water, but they finally found the pod of whales they were looking for. Brian jumped in and joined these beasts of the sea in their natural habitat.

The whales were as majestic as he had hoped, but as they swam away, things quickly went wrong. As Brian swam back to the boat, a group of poisonous jellyfish surrounded him, stinging him around 300 times from head to toe.

The three-hour return journey was made worse because the island had no hospital. He was literally in the middle of nowhere with no idea of what to do.

Brian barely survived the night—alone and without electricity, vomiting and burning with fever, he lay awake praying that the Lord would help him in his great need. As morning dawned, the only place he could think to go to was the local church. Finding the pastor, he asked him to pray that God would heal his body.

With tears filling his eyes, Brian told me of how the pastor laid his hands on him and prayed. What came next seemed almost unbelievable. As they prayed, Brian initially felt, and then saw, a lump travel around his body before leaving through his stomach.

And with that, the poison was gone.

Ye of little faith?

My first reaction was a mixture of joy and disbelief. Joy to know that he was okay, but disbelief as to whether this kind of supernatural occurrence was possible.

If this had happened where I live, Brian would have been within reach of a hospital. Would he have gone to a pastor? It's unlikely. He probably would have called an ambulance and prayed. He would have been seen by doctors, who would have known how to treat him and have had access to antidotes for the poison that filled his body.

Is one response more faithful, or even more spiritual, than another? Not necessarily. God is equally in both scenarios.

Healing and mental illness

God's ongoing grace for us means we have a wide variety of resources at our disposal. In the West, there is an abundance of available medications and health-care professionals. These are gracious provisions which, when used wisely, can be of great help in our journey to find healing.

God can be as much in the pastor's healing hands as he is in the doctor's training. Both positions can be abused and used foolishly, but they can also be used to bring about mercy and goodness.

The kind of healing Brian experienced can and does still happen in the Western world. We must not underestimate prayer when something goes wrong in our bodies and minds. But we need to also remember to thank and credit God when he works through doctors, psychologists and other health professionals. In these, also, we can find answers to our prayers.

God of the "ordinary"

On the very day of writing this, I came across a video which explored the disillusionment with 21st-century living—the fact that we are wealthier and more educated than ever, while at the same time increasingly unhappy and dissatisfied. The video went on to conclude that the rise in use of antidepressants is a sign that we are becoming more disconnected from God.

As somebody who has been on medication for a number of years, this kind of sentiment makes me uneasy to say the least. The message communicated—that antide-pressants are only needed by those who are separated from God—can leave those of us who genuinely benefit from this kind of treatment feeling spiritually inferior.

When my psychiatrist (a Christian, incidentally), pre-scribed me antidepressants, she determined that there was a chemical imbalance in my brain. The recommend-ed medication has since become a great blessing and contributor to my overall wellbeing. It is not the only form of treatment I receive, but it has played an import-ant part in my recovery. I am grateful to God for it.

Our gospel identity tells us that we are in right relation-ship with God through Christ alone. It is not based on who we are, or what we do or do not do. This means that God's view of us never changes. He knows what we are going through and his love is unending. Christ lived our kind of pain, suffering and weakness, and he does not leave us alone.

God is in all of his world, providing blessing for the creation he loves dearly. He is not just our Creator and Saviour but our Sustainer as well. It is God who gives intellect to the scientist and insight to the psychologist. Science and psychology will always be flawed in a broken world, but there is still goodness to many of the innovations in these areas. Whether we acknowledge it or not, God is in everything—even the ordinary.

God of the "extraordinary"

This is not to say there isn't a place for more "supernatural" healing in mental illness. I believe God can relieve us of depression and anxiety in the same way he relieved Brian of the jellyfish's poison. We can confidently believe that God is capable of doing all things, and so it is right for us to ask him to take away the pain of depression and anxiety.

> *Now you are the body of Christ, and each one of you is a part of it. And God has placed in the church first of all apostles, second prophets, third teachers, then miracles, then gifts of healing, of helping, of guidance, and of different kinds of tongues. Are all apostles? Are all prophets? Are all teachers? Do all work miracles? Do all have gifts of healing? Do all speak in tongues? Do all interpret? Now eagerly desire the greater gifts.*
>
> 1 CORINTHIANS 12 V 27-31

This passage can cause division due to the role and presence of spiritual gifts. But if we hold a high view of Scripture, we can confidently conclude from these verses that healing happens and is a gift from God when exercised in love (1 Corinthians 13). To assume that every Christian will be healed is to try and predict what God will do. His actions cannot be predicted. But at the same time, we can pray in confidence, knowing that God can heal.

God is in all

Whether in the seemingly supernatural, or the seemingly ordinary, God is present. He is able to work through the Christian and non-Christian alike. This is why Jesus can say:

> *You have heard that it was said, "Love your neighbour and hate your enemy." But I tell you, love your enemies and pray for those who persecute you, that you may be children of your Father in heaven. He causes his sun to rise on the evil and the good, and sends rain on the righteous and the unrighteous.* MATTHEW 5 V 43-45

God causes the sun to rise and the rain to fall on Christians and non-Christians alike. In the same way, he gives intellect and insight to all of his creation. It is God who gives the doctor their intellect. It is God who gives the psychologist an awareness of how the brain functions. It is God who gives the laboratory scientist the insight to invent new medication. In his mercy, God loves and blesses all of his creation.

In our sinfulness we do not always use our gifts for good. The doctor can be bribed to prescribe only a certain brand of medication. The psychologist can care little for the patient and fail to understand their needs. The scientist can use their skills to create illicit and harmful drugs. Because of this, it is right to show careful discernment (more on this in chapter 11, page 91).

What if he does neither?

But what if God does neither? What if you do not experience supernatural healing, and you cannot find a medication or treatment that seems to work? What then?

This can be painful to experience, but it does not change what the Bible tells us about God. The truth is, there is so much we do not understand about God and his plans. But he has revealed enough of himself for us to know how deeply he loves us—that he is for us and not against us (Romans 8 v 31-32). We must hold tightly to this core truth when we feel as if he's not listening or doesn't care.

It can be deeply dissatisfying not to know why God chooses to do, or not do, certain things. Why does one person find an effective treatment and another doesn't? Why does one person receive supernatural healing, while the other prays with no change?

We have always wanted the mind of God—this was the promise that Satan falsely offered Adam and Eve. But the truth is, sometimes we just don't know. And this is why a gospel identity is at the core of who we are. When we don't know why, we can be confident of God's love. How? Because he did not even spare his own Son in his desire to save you and me.

Ongoing suffering is a burden I do not wish on anybody. At the same time, know that it does not change the goodness and love of God. Rather, we keep our eyes fixed on the day when God will restore his creation, including us, once and for all. What a beautiful day that will be.

For reflection

God's ways cannot be predicted, but they must not be underestimated either. Have you prayed to God to deliver you from your depression and anxiety? What are the resources he has placed in your life that you are blessed with? Will your gospel identity be taken away if you are not healed from mental illness?

CHAPTER 11
DISCERNMENT

You get what you get...

Every parent has their favourites clichés: "Life's not fair", "Not while you're living under my roof", and of course, the unanswerable, "Because I said so".

I used to groan every time I heard one of them. Now, as a parent of four young kids, I'm quickly turning into what I once deplored.

My own cliché of choice is, "You get what you get and you don't get upset".

I have found this line particularly effective at the dinner table. Complaints can range from different meal sizes through to who got the pink plate.

Sometimes in life we just get what we get. When I was admitted to hospital, I was immediately assigned an in-house psychiatrist. It was their job to examine my current medication, ask a set of assessment questions, and determine an appropriate course of action during my stay.

I had no choice in who my psychiatrist would be: no say in their age or gender, and definitely not in their religious affiliation. On this occasion, when my psychiatrist found out I was a pastor in training, she shared that she was herself a Christian. I was grateful to the Lord for giving me a Christian psychiatrist, but this certainly wasn't true of all the professionals at the hospital.

During group counselling, the approach or advice given by in-house psychologists indicated little of an allegiance to Christ. After all, this was not their role. One such example was when I was told to cut a particular person out of my life because of the negative impact they were having on me. It was not an abusive relationship—just one that caused me frustration. As a Christian, I chose not to adopt this advice. I don't believe this is what it means to love my neighbour as myself.

Choices

Of course we don't always have to just get what we get. Often we have choice. And as Christians, when we do have a choice, we have a question to consider: should we only see Christian professionals?

Prior to my hospital stay, I had seen Christian counsellors. But when I became a student at Bible college, I simply couldn't afford to pay the full amount for their consultations. I then found a psychologist who charged a reduced amount. She was not a Christian, but gave me some incredibly helpful advice, and I am still very grateful for her generosity in this way. Perhaps you've been faced with a similar choice.

All things being equal

Let's assume that you are given the choice of seeing two psychologists. Both have the same training and experience. Who do you choose? It's difficult to know. Without any further information, you may just have to pick one at random.

Now let's say that one is a Christian and one is not. Who do you choose? I would recommend first trying the Christian. Why? Because while there are no guarantees, the Christian professional is more likely to provide guidance that is more in line with the Bible's teaching.

This is very important when we are experiencing depression or anxiety. In our fragility, we can be desperate to find answers. Seeing a Christian professional increases the chance that these answers will be in accordance with Scripture.

But choosing a Christian professional does not guarantee a biblically authentic perspective. For example, I have met people who have told me how Christian psychologists encouraged them to pursue divorce when there was very little biblical basis for doing so.

Seeking Christian counsel should probably be our default option, but it's not a guarantee and we must have room to be flexible.

Things aren't always equal

When I saw the non-Christian psychologist, my alternatives were not equal. At the time, I was presented with two options. The first, a Christian professional who charged a fee I couldn't afford. The other, a non-Christian professional who offered a discounted rate. If money had been no issue, I would have chosen the Christian. But money was an issue, and I decided it was better to get some help than none.

Aside from cost, one of the key reasons we need to be flexible is because of access. I live in a city of 5 million people. There are many services at my disposal. For others who live in more remote areas or with fewer social services, there just may not be that choice. I believe if the best professional help you can access comes from a non-Christian, then you would be wise to choose this rather than to receive no help at all.

There is goodness in the world

When we ask whether it's appropriate for a Christian to see a non-Christian professional, it's helpful to remember again that God is in all of his creation. It's God who gives intellect to the psychologist as much as he does to the theologian. He can, and does, work through all people in his world, not just through those who declare him to be their Lord.

A Christian can engage with secular psychology because God has been gracious enough to give even those who are not believers insight and expertise. If the best psychologist you have access to claims no allegiance to Christ, they can still be of great value. Like you and I, they are still made in God's image, and have the ability to bring profound blessing.

But it isn't perfect

However, as Christians, we shouldn't blindly assume that every word of a psychologist (whether Christian or non-Christian) ought to be adopted.

We may disagree with certain perspectives, but that does not mean we have to withdraw from secular psychology completely. The consequences of the fall should never surprise us, and so we aren't shocked when we are presented with teaching contrary to God's word. Instead, we are daily faced with choices to live in line with, or against, God's will for our lives. So we respond to secular psychology carefully and prayerfully, asking God to help us see what is good and comes from him, and what we need to say no to.

So be discerning

So how are we to be discerning? First, we grow in deeper knowledge and love of God's word. Knowing God allows us to say yes at certain times and no at others. He has shown himself in the truths of Scripture. We can take confidence in the Spirit to remind and convict us of this truth, and so we don't have to rely on our own wisdom to work out the difference between right and wrong. Like Paul, we can pray for discernment (Philippians 1 v 10).

If you are new in your faith, or there are areas of advice you feel unsure about, it may be helpful to sit down with a pastor or Christian mentor and examine what has been discussed in a counselling session. God gives us his word, and he also gives us one another to help live out the truths of Scripture.

One of the beauties of the gospel story is that it isn't confined to God joining us for 33 years in the first century. No, he continues to dwell with us to this day. The Father did not cease to be active at the completion of creation, nor did the Son cease to be active when he ascended into heaven. Rather, we have a God who is an ongoing presence in our lives through the Holy Spirit. This gives us great comfort, for we realise that God in his great mercy has not left us to navigate life alone. He is with us at all times, and he will not desert us.

If you love me, keep my commands. And I will ask the Father, and he will give you another advocate to help you and be with you forever—the Spirit of truth. The world cannot accept him, because it neither sees him

*nor knows him. But you know him, for he lives with
you and will be in you. I will not leave you as orphans;
I will come to you. Before long, the world will not see
me anymore, but you will see me. Because I live, you
also will live. On that day you will realise that I am
in my Father, and you are in me, and I am in you.
Whoever has my commands and keeps them is the one
who loves me. The one who loves me will be loved by
my Father, and I too will love them and show myself to
them.*   JOHN 14 V 15-21

This passage teaches us that as believers, both individually and collectively, we have God's Spirit to help us see the world through his eyes. Therefore we should expect to see things differently from the world around us.

Jesus tells his disciples that he will not leave them as orphans. God has been present from the beginning of time, and he continues to be with us right up to the present day.

We do not need to separate ourselves from the world we live in. Rather, we can engage in God's world with confidence. We have not been left alone. We know the truth. If we run to God's word, and share in this with trusted brothers and sisters, we will daily learn how to become more and more like him. When we receive advice from professionals, we can filter what we hear through what we learn in Scripture.

We are vulnerable

Our gospel identity tells us that ultimate love is found in Christ. We can trust God. Immersing ourselves in Scripture is no boring obligation. Trusting in God's Spirit is not just a practice for the hyper-emotional. Keeping ourselves in tune with God is a privilege that allows us to find direction and stability. When I am unwell, all I want is to get better. This places me in a position of vulnerability if I do not have God to help me distinguish sound from unsound advice. Without a foundation in the Lord, I am like a leaf blowing in the wind, ready to be tossed in every direction.

But if we recognise our vulnerability, we can ask the Lord to protect us and show us the wise way forward. When we trust in God's revealed truth, we are able to seek help from both Christian and non-Christian professionals, while remaining firmly grounded in God's perfect love and will for our lives. We can trust him to work both through his word and also his created world.

For reflection

What professional resources do you have at your disposal that can assist in your recovery and healing? How will your knowledge of God impact what you do with the advice you receive?

CHAPTER 12
PRAYER

Wailing and the West

I'm struck when I watch the news by just how much heartache occurs in the world every day. This can be an extra challenge to those of us who are already struggling with the pain in our own lives.

I've noticed that whether it be a terrorist attack or natural disaster, responses to suffering seem to differ greatly around the world.

In the West, even the death of a loved one can carry unspoken expectations that we will "keep it together". If we need to scream, we do it behind closed doors, if at all.

This is in stark contrast to what I often see on the news. In the Middle East particularly, wailing for loved ones seems to be quite acceptable, and even normal. To me, this seems to be a more fitting response to the loss of someone we love. Suffering hurts, and yet we don't like to show it in the West.

A culturally-influenced prayer life

I wonder how these kinds of cultural expectations influence the way we pray. Do we try to hide our pain from God? Mental illness can cause times of despair and grief, but do we believe we can express this in our faith? We may not think we can be real with God—even though he's the one who already intimately knows our hearts and minds, so he already knows exactly how we feel.

The Bible contains many prayers where God's children plainly tell him of their anguish in times of need. In Jeremiah 20, tired of the constant rejection and mocking he receives, the prophet Jeremiah tells God exactly how he feels. And it isn't comfortable:

> *You deceived me, Lord, and I was deceived;*
> *you overpowered me and prevailed.*
> *I am ridiculed all day long;*
> *everyone mocks me.*
> *Whenever I speak, I cry out*
> *proclaiming violence and destruction.*
> *So the word of the Lord has brought me*
> *insult and reproach all day long.*
>
> Jeremiah 20 v 7-8

Jeremiah's prayer is astonishing. He is so bold that he claims the Lord has deceived him. The Hebrew word in verse 7 (translated as "deceived") can also mean "persuaded", but even so, Jeremiah is clearly saying the Lord made him do something he didn't want to do.

This was not the life he had signed up for. Jeremiah, the son of a priest, had been heading for a life of respect in the religious world of Israel. But God had other plans, and Jeremiah didn't like it. His ministry would instead be marked with warning an unrepentant generation of God's coming judgment.

And yet, in the very same prayer, Jeremiah continues with these words:

But the LORD is with me like a mighty warrior;
so my persecutors will stumble and not prevail.
They will fail and be thoroughly disgraced;
their dishonour will never be forgotten.
LORD Almighty, you who examine the righteous
and probe the heart and mind,
let me see your vengeance on them,
for to you I have committed my cause.

Sing to the LORD!
Give praise to the Lord!
He rescues the life of the needy
from the hands of the wicked.

JEREMIAH 20 V 11-13

How is it that Jeremiah can transition so quickly from despair to praise? Because he has a robust relationship with the Lord. Like any deep relationship, there will be times of conflict and times of harmony.

And so, once more, in the same prayer, Jeremiah's tone changes greatly:

> *Cursed be the day I was born!*
> *May the day my mother bore me not be blessed!*
> *Cursed be the man who brought my father the news,*
> *who made him very glad, saying,*
> *"A child is born to you—a son!"*
> *May that man be like the towns*
> *the LORD overthrew without pity.*
> *May he hear wailing in the morning,*
> *a battle cry at noon.*
> *For he did not kill me in the womb,*
> *with my mother as my grave,*
> *her womb enlarged for ever.*
> *Why did I ever come out of the womb*
> *to see trouble and sorrow*
> *and to end my days in shame?*
>
> JEREMIAH 20 v 14-18

This is not a nice, pleasant or polite prayer. It doesn't follow Western expectations of relationship. It's painfully honest both in its declarations of praise and deep lament. Jeremiah concludes by cursing both the day he was born and the person who delivered the news of his birth.

This is wailing aloud more than screaming into a pillow. So why is it included in Scripture? What is the Lord showing us?

Free to be real

If you are in Christ, you have the freedom to pray this kind of prayer. I wouldn't lightly recommend that you curse the day you were born to the one who has given you life. But at the same time, God already knows what's on your heart, and so expressing how you truly feel comes as no surprise to him. Know this—your relationship with the Lord is real. Like any real relationship, there will be ups and downs.

We don't have to tiptoe around God. But the question is will we, like Jeremiah, still declare God's praises if things don't go our way?

Our call is to worship the Lord in times of plenty and in times of need. This means you can:

- *Praise him* with all your heart, because you know he has rescued you from death.

- *Cry out to him* with all your heart, because Christ knows the pain of being human in a fallen world.

Wailing without cursing

Let's not forget who we're praying to. When the prophet Isaiah directly comes before God (Isaiah 6), he is completely broken in awe of him. When the glory of God comes before Moses, his face becomes radiant (Exodus 34 v 29-35). *God is God, and we are not.*

How then can we be real in suffering while aware that we also stand in the presence of the almighty God? The answer lies not in whether we acknowledge our pain, but whether we curse God because of this pain.

Jeremiah may have gone too far—it's a controversial verse, and personally, I'm not sure one way or another. He curses the day he was born but does not directly curse God.

However, there is another instance in the Bible where we see the line most definitely crossed. In Job chapter 2, when everything seems to be falling apart, Job's wife speaks:

> *His wife said to him, "Are you still maintaining your integrity? Curse God and die!"* Job 2 v 9

Job's wife believes his suffering should lead to a cursing of God. Their children, servants and livestock have died. But Job is described as a righteous man without blame (Job 1 v 1), and so, he wisely rejects the advice of his wife. In chapter 30, we see Job's raw and honest lament. But he also knows the line between being real and being disrespectful:

> *I cry out to you, God, but you do not answer;*
>   *I stand up, but you merely look at me.*
> *You turn on me ruthlessly;*
>   *with the might of your hand you attack me.*
> *You snatch me up and drive me before the wind;*
>   *you toss me about in the storm.*
> *I know you will bring me down to death,*
>   *to the place appointed for all the living.*

JOB 30 V 20-23

God never tells Job why he suffers. Chapters 40 – 42 contain God's lengthy and awe-inspiring response. *God is God. Job is not.* That much he makes clear. At the same time, the Bible does not claim that Job has lost his righteous standing. As close to the line as Job treads, even the prayer above is that of a righteous man in a time of great suffering.

God knows pain

With a gospel identity we can go further than acknowledging that God has saved us from the pain of this fallen world. Hebrews 4 tells us that God also *joined* us in the world. His love for us runs so deep that he doesn't just feel sorrow for our pain. No, he takes on our pain.

Therefore, since we have a great high priest who has ascended into heaven, Jesus the Son of God, let us hold firmly to the faith we profess. For we do not have a high priest who is unable to feel sympathy for our weaknesses, but we have one who has been tempted in every way, just as we are—yet he did not sin. Let us then approach God's throne of grace with confidence, so that we may receive mercy and find grace to help us in our time of need. HEBREWS 4 V 14-16

You may feel like cursing God in the anguish of your mental illness, but this is not the right response. Groan—yes. Mourn—yes. Wail—yes.

Curse—no.

There is no sense in cursing the only one who truly frees you from your pain—the one who knows exactly what it's like. Christ does not just theoretically understand suffering. He willingly experienced it for you and me.

So we are free to both praise God and cry out to him. We don't need to hide things from him, or try and dress them up. We can come to the Lord as we are.

For reflection

How much does your prayer life reflect the expectations that your culture places on relationships? In the midst of depression and anxiety, you are free to express the full range of your feelings. At the same time, remember that God is holy and not to be cursed for your suffering.

CHAPTER 13
GUARANTEES

We love guarantees. They provide a safety net against uncertainty. We want to know that if our car breaks down, it will be fixed under warranty. We want the assurance of receiving our money back if we aren't completely satisfied with a product. We know we can trust a true friend to always deliver on a promise.

But what about God? What does he guarantee, and not guarantee, if our identity is in Christ? Where is our safety net in the gospel?

Gospel guarantees

Let's start with what we can be assured of. If you're in Christ, you have the greatest guarantee of all—your place in eternity has been secured through the death and resurrection of your Saviour. There can be no greater joy. God guarantees that his love will never cease and that his mercies will never end. We may not always feel the fullness of this joy, but this can't take away the reality of what God has given to us.

Over the years, I've had the privilege of seeing people come to Christ, and one of the passages I like to begin with is from Romans 10:

> *If you declare with your mouth, "Jesus is Lord," and*
> *believe in your heart that God raised him from the*
> *dead, you will be saved.*   ROMANS 10 V 9

In the midst of some of the most dense theology in all of Scripture, this verse is beautifully simple. It's a guarantee. Paul doesn't say you might be saved, or you will only be saved if God is feeling generous on a particular day. No—Paul says you *will* be saved if you believe that Jesus is Lord and God raised him from the dead.

I've seen this verse bring peace, when people realise they are not condemned or trapped in their sin. For others, its simplicity has been a barrier in coming to faith. One man told me, "It's too easy", and so this verse became a stumbling block for him.

Both responses come from a realisation that our faith is unmistakably simple at its core. The gospel is beautiful because it guarantees to us God's unwavering love in the midst of our own shortcomings.

Gospel non-guarantees

If God loves us, why then can Christians still experience anxiety and depression?

The simple answer is that disciples of Christ remain in the midst of a broken world. We look forward to a day with no more crying and no more pain (Revelation 21 v 4). But that day has not yet arrived. Until then, we are guaranteed God's love but not a life of ease.

If God is for us, who can be against us? He who did not spare his own Son, but gave him up for us all—how will he not also, along with him, graciously give us all things? Who will bring any charge against those whom God has chosen? It is God who justifies. Who then is the one who condemns? No one. Christ Jesus who died—more than that, who was raised to life—is at the right hand of God and is also interceding for us. Who shall separate us from the love of Christ? Shall trouble or hardship or persecution or famine or nakedness or danger or sword? As it is written:

"For your sake we face death all day long;
* we are considered as sheep to be slaughtered."*

No, in all these things we are more than conquerors through him who loved us. For I am convinced that neither death nor life, neither angels nor demons, neither the present nor the future, nor any powers, neither height nor depth, nor anything else in all creation, will be able to separate us from the love of God that is in Christ Jesus our Lord.

ROMANS 8 v 31-39

Notice what Paul does and doesn't say here. He unashamedly declares that if God is for us, no one can be against us. And yet he goes on to list a series of hardships that Christians can expect to find.

Paul does not say that we're immune from trouble, hardship, persecution, famine, nakedness, danger or sword. What he does say is that in the midst of all these things, we cannot be separated from the love of God that is in Christ Jesus. God's love for his people is guaranteed.

We shouldn't be surprised

God delights in granting us daily blessings—food, family, friends, jobs, sunshine and rain. His mercies are new every day and it's important for us to recognise his loving hand. At the same time, we cannot expect perfection simply because we're Christians. Quite the opposite—our understanding of a world that is broken leads us to expect suffering.

Christians can make two errors here. The first is to believe that we're entitled to all the promises of the new creation in the present day—material prosperity, health and harmony. The problem with this is that it gives us no framework for suffering. Worse still, it can lead us to believe that God doesn't love us when we do suffer. But this isn't true. The Romans 8 passage above makes it clear that we can expect suffering—and that it does **not** mean we have lost God's love.

But we should also remember that God does delight to bless us in this life. And in this remembering, we can find delight in even the little things. Those of us who wrestle with mental illness must keep fighting to remember these blessings, especially when depression or anxiety make it harder for us to do so. These are the times when we pray that the Lord will make his blessings especially clear.

If we trust that God loves us, we can find meaning in this life. If God loves us, we can expect him to bless us as an outpouring of his grace and mercy. But if we expect every blessing in *this* life, we have lost sight of the perfection that will be ours in the new creation. Or, as Paul puts it earlier in Romans 8:

We know that the whole creation has been groaning as in the pains of childbirth right up to the present time. Not only so, but we ourselves, who have the firstfruits of the Spirit, groan inwardly as we wait eagerly for our adoption to sonship, the redemption of our bodies. For in this hope we were saved. But hope that is seen is no hope at all. Who hopes for what they already have? But if we hope for what we do not yet have, we wait for it patiently. ROMANS 8 v 22-25

Depression and anxiety will cause us to suffer, but God's love is guaranteed. It's this love that continues to grant us blessing in this life. And it's this love that assures us of the final peace that will be ours in the new creation.

For reflection

Is the love of God proved false if Christians experience mental illness? (See Lamentations 3 v 19-33.) What is it that God does, and does not, guarantee us in the gospel?

CHAPTER 14
COMMUNITY

Favourite shows

In my house, only a few TV shows are on the "unmissable" list. For the kids, *Peppa Pig* is right at the top. My tastes are slightly different, though there will always be a place in my heart for animated talking animals.

My wife, Lara, and I prefer lifestyle shows, especially *Grand Designs*. Each episode takes the viewer through a unique home-renovation or construction. Some are large, others small, and all have plenty of hurdles to overcome.

My favourite episode involves a building co-operative on a tight budget. Ten families learn different trades in order to build one another's homes. The end result? After much turmoil, a community of people who are able to enjoy permanent shelter, each other's company and the labour of their hands. The concept intrigued me because of the blessing this kind of community life promised.

God's grand design

As I look at Scripture, I believe that community must similarly be an important part of the church's DNA. It doesn't have to look like living next door to one another, but according to the Bible, community must look like something.

We see community right from the beginning. The Bible's grand design begins with God himself, before any of us were made. God exists in the triune relationship—Father, Son and Spirit. He is in community with himself. Then Adam is made (Genesis 2 v 7) in God's image (1 v 27), but God soon confronts Adam with the fact of his loneliness (2 v 19-20). Before the fall, all that God makes is "good" and "very good". And yet, the Lord acknowledges that it's "not good" for the man to be alone (Genesis 2 v 18). So God creates the woman, and there's an instant bond when Adam and Eve come together (Genesis 2 v 22-23).

In a broken world

After the fall, we see how community now carries a dark side. In Genesis 4, Cain murders Abel. Two chapters later, God laments the wickedness of the human race so much that he sends the flood. By the end of Genesis 11, God has disperses mankind throughout the world at Babel because of how they use community for their own sinful desires.

The story continues.

Joseph's brothers sell him into slavery because of jealousy (Genesis 37). The people of God prostitute themselves with foreign spouses and the idols they worship (1 Kings 11; Ezekiel 8). Judas Iscariot, one of Jesus' trusted friends, betrays him and hands him over for crucifixion (Luke 22). Relationships can be good, but they can also be very, very broken.

Once bitten, twice shy?

It would be easy to give up on community because of broken relationships. But Jesus didn't. In Matthew 26, we read how Peter denied Jesus three times. Christ knew this would happen—he even predicted it. And yet, just ten chapters earlier, Jesus had given Peter perhaps the greatest responsibility a person has ever been given.

Peter had just discovered who Jesus is—that he is the promised Christ or Messiah: God's chosen King. In response, Jesus tells Peter:

> *Blessed are you, Simon son of Jonah, for this was not revealed to you by flesh and blood, but by my Father in heaven. And I tell you that you are Peter, and on this rock I will build my church, and the gates of Hades will not overcome it.*   MATTHEW 16 v 17-18

Jesus gives Peter a massive role in the future church. And yet, just five verses later, Jesus calls Peter "Satan"!

Why? Because Peter had just denied that the Christ must suffer and die. In the ups and downs of Peter's life, Jesus shows that imperfect people and relationships have never stopped God from believing in the importance of his church.

It's more than a human institution; we're told in Hebrews that the church is also a vital part of running the race of faith until the very end:

> *Let us hold unswervingly to the hope we profess, for he who promised is faithful. And let us consider how we may spur one another on towards love and good deeds, not giving up meeting together, as some are in the habit of doing, but encouraging one another—and all the more as you see the Day approaching.*
>
> HEBREWS 10 V 23-25

A desire to flee

I'm naturally an extrovert who normally has no problem in sharing my life with others. Despite this, I remember not wanting a single visitor while I was in hospital, apart from my wife. I didn't want my church to know. I didn't want to have to explain the situation or how it could have come to this. I didn't want to be asked how I was going. I wanted to be left alone, because I felt so alone.

And I'm an extrovert.

What if you don't share my personality type? What if you know that a great knot in your stomach is only a Sunday service away? What if you don't want to be asked for another prayer point because you don't feel any better? Or how do you respond when a loved one is in the midst of depression or anxiety, and doesn't want to engage with you or anyone else in the church about it?

It is very common for those of us who struggle with depression or anxiety to find community difficult. This applies to all communities, but it is a particular challenge when it comes to church. As Christians we know we are called to meet together—and yet there are times when this feels close to impossible.

A shared need

This is an area where those of us who live with mental illness need to be willing to challenge ourselves. We don't need to be ashamed of how we feel, but it's important that we persevere. The message of Hebrews 10 is unashamed in saying that we need to help one another if we're going to run the race set before us until the very end. So being part of the church family isn't just about how we feel; it's also where we encourage others as we live the Christian life together.

The gospel reminds us that we're all in need and have an ongoing dependence on Christ. God doesn't just love us when we're easy to love. He doesn't desire our achievements, performance or credentials. He desires *us.* Finding others within the church who can exhibit that same kind of love will be a great blessing in your times of need. An extrovert will probably end up feeling more comfortable sharing some of their struggles. An introvert probably won't, but will still benefit from finding a handful of brothers and sisters who understand and have compassion on you in your time of need.

Asking and receiving

We have a saying in our church that "we never want anyone to suffer alone". We also have more than 1000 adults and youth in our community. So, often, we need people to tell us if they're struggling, for us to be able to help. You may feel you want to isolate yourself, but in many ways this simply leaves you alone with your thoughts and feelings. Telling even just a couple of people can be a great help in your faith.

Do you have anxiety about not having anyone to sit with? If you don't tell anyone, you may not receive the support you need. Would someone driving you to church or your small group help motivate you to go? You may need to ask someone who lives in your area. Do you need to step down from an area of ministry? Tell someone who you know won't judge you for it.

And if you're the person to whom someone comes for help, please remember that it takes a lot of courage for them to do so. They're admitting their fragility, and that isn't easy for anyone. Listen to them. Seek to understand them. And most of all, remember you're just as dependent on the loving grace of God as they are. You've been asked for help because they trust and respect you, and so honour them by faithfully carrying that responsibility.

Dear friends, since God so loved us, we also ought to love one another. No one has ever seen God; but if we love one another, God lives in us and his love is made complete in us.   I JOHN 4 V 11-12

The importance of a loving community

In my own walk with depression, and in my time in pastoral ministry, I've observed some common traits that make for good counsel in times of need:

Trust

The first principle is trust. This means finding people who you believe can keep what you tell them confidential. And if you're the one in the support role, it's critical to honour the sensitivity of the situation. The one exception to this may be if you think the person is at risk of harm. Otherwise, mutual trust and a promise not to gossip about what has been said are vital.

Loving truth

Truth is important as it allows for the challenging of thoughts, feelings and behaviours. But without love, truth becomes brash and arrogant. When spoken in love, truth becomes gentle and nurturing.

Choosing someone who will be honest and compassionate at the same time means they will likely have your best interests at heart. This could be a trusted Christian friend, a counsellor, or your pastor.

Speaking honestly if you're the one doing the caring can be hard, as you may be worried about causing offence. Pointing a loved one back to Scripture with passages such as Hebrews 10 will mean you speak with God's wisdom and not simply your own.

You also have an opportunity to remind a loved one that church provides an opportunity for every believer to play a significant role in the work of Christ. Mental illness does not exclude us from the important part each believer has:

> *The eye cannot say to the hand, "I don't need you!"*
> *And the head cannot say to the feet, "I don't need you!"*
> *On the contrary, those parts of the body that seem to be*
> *weaker are indispensable, and the parts that we think*
> *are less honourable we treat with special honour.*
>
> 1 Corinthians 12 v 21-23

Wisdom

Finally, wisdom is built into the ability to speak truth in love. When I think of someone who's wise, I picture a person who can sift through conflicting or difficult information. A wise person speaks, but only when there is something worth saying. Wise counsel is able to listen without judgment. A wise person may give concrete advice, but they will also provide principles to help a person work through issues themselves.

If you are the carer, and you worry that you may lack the wisdom you need, then ask the Lord to provide for you. As you bring the person you are caring for before the Lord in prayer, he will help you know what and what not to say as you care for them and point them back to Christ. That's why James encourages us to ask God for the wisdom we need:

> *If any of you lacks wisdom, you should ask God, who gives generously to all without finding fault, and it will be given to you.* JAMES I V 5

For reflection

The community God gives us is a blessing. If you struggle with church, who can you ask to help you, and what kind of help will be most useful? How can each of us in the church love one another in the way we are called to?

CHAPTER 15
LOVE

A zig-zagging journey

Two days before being discharged from hospital, I was shown a graph of what to expect when returning to the "outside world". I was encouraged that the picture was one of hopeful recovery. But rather than tracking progress as a steady uphill slope, the diagram appeared more like a zig-zagging mountain landscape, where the peaks gradually became higher and more frequent.

The point of the exercise was to show that for anyone living with depression and anxiety, the journey would be full of ups and downs. While it's so important to celebrate progress, we also shouldn't be surprised by difficult days, weeks or even months.

Reading for one you love

At the beginning of this book, I mentioned that you may be interested not for yourself, but because someone close to you is living with depression or anxiety. Thank you. The more you can do to understand their situation, the greater your impact can be. This chapter is especially for you.

There are so many things that can be said on how to care for someone you love. In fact, there is probably a whole other book to be written on that very topic. But for this one chapter, allow me to give you a single guiding principle. Whether a spouse, family member or friend, you may be wondering how to care for someone you love. And in that question lies the answer. You love them.

Love is...

If there was ever a classic Bible passage on love, 1 Corinthians 13 must be it. It's always a favourite at weddings, but the original context is actually speaking of mutual love between brothers and sisters in the church:

Love is patient, love is kind. It does not envy, it does not boast, it is not proud. It does not dishonour others, it is not self-seeking, it is not easily angered, it keeps no record of wrongs. Love does not delight in evil but rejoices with the truth. It always protects, always trusts, always hopes, always perseveres.

1 Corinthians 13 v 4-7

Every characteristic of love in this passage is first found in the Lord. The gospel itself is a message of love—of a God who is so gripped by his love for a world that rejects him that he has given his own Son for them.

1 Corinthians 13 shows that love is many things. Notice what it doesn't say, though—that love is *easy*. Godly self-sacrifice rarely comes naturally to us. But if you really want to know how best to care for someone with anxiety and depression, consider these verses.

Patience

What the zig-zagging diagram in hospital gave me was a framework to know what to expect. I was in for a journey, and it was going to take time. It's a journey that I'm still on, and it may well be a lifelong one.

While each aspect of love in 1 Corinthians 13 has profound implications, I want to focus specifically on the importance of *patient love.*

In many ways, the story of the Bible is one of God's unending, patient love for his people. Nehemiah chapter 9 is a powerful passage which tells of God's faithfulness in the face of Israel's wickedness:

> *But they, our ancestors, became arrogant and stiff-necked, and they did not obey your commands. They refused to listen and failed to remember the miracles you performed among them. They became stiff-necked and in their rebellion appointed a leader in order to return to their slavery. But you are a forgiving God,* **gracious and compassionate, slow to anger and abounding in love.** *Therefore you did not desert them, even when they cast for themselves an image of a calf and said, 'This is your god, who brought you up out of Egypt,' or when they committed awful blasphemies.*
>
> NEHEMIAH 9 v 16-18 *(bold text mine)*

This passage is just one of many that use this wonderful phrase to describe our Lord: "gracious and compassionate, slow to anger and abounding in love" (see also Exodus 34 v 6; Numbers 14 v 18; Joel 2 v 13; Jonah 4 v 2; as well as several of the psalms).

God's character is one of loving patience for each of us, no matter who we are or what illness we do or don't live with. It's a love that stretches beyond days, weeks and months, and even generations.

God could have done away with sin by being done with us. Instead, he has chosen to end the curse of sin through the blood of his own Son. This is love at its most unbelievably generous.

What does that mean for us? If we've received the loving patience of God, let's in kind show the same loving patience to those around us.

You'd go to the doctor for a broken leg...

You may have heard this said before. It's a well-meaning sentiment that attempts to break the stigma of mental illness. The point is that if we feel comfortable enough to seek medical help for a physical aliment, such as a broken leg, then we should feel the same for a mental one.

Even though I appreciate the intention behind the illustration, I always felt uneasy about it, although I could never work out why. Then, a friend who's a nurse helped me put my finger on the problem. She explained the difference between *acute* and *chronic* illnesses. Some ailments have a specific timeframe of recovery (acute), while others are indefinite (chronic).

There was my answer. If you break your leg, you can expect to be on crutches for 6 to 8 weeks. After that, you'll probably be back to walking and running as before. But if you're living with depression or anxiety, you don't get a specific timeframe. You don't know how long it's going to impact your life. It could ease after a few weeks or months—but it may not.

In the same way, if you decide you want to take a caring role in a loved one's life, you should expect a chronic, indefinite timescale. This isn't to say that mental illness will inevitably last a lifetime, although it may. Rather, you need to emotionally prepare yourself for a long-term investment in somebody's life.

Love is patient.

When we care for someone who is mentally ill, we can easily feel the pressure to "save" that person. So we think it's our responsibility to make them better, and that it's our fault if they don't recover. But however much you love them, you cannot become their saviour. And you don't need to! Your role is to patiently love them, and point them to the Lord. He is the true Saviour—not you.

Whatever you're feeling, I'm probably feeling it even more

If receiving patient love is on one end of the spectrum, then feeling pressure from others to get better is on the other. As a depressive, feeling stuck inside my own mind can be a scary space to be. Believe me, if I could figure out a quick or easy way to get better, I'd take it! But there isn't one—and I can't.

While there's certainly some scope to challenge the thoughts, feelings and actions of loved ones, if your desire is to "fix them", then you will likely be left very frustrated, and so will they.

Your loved one is probably already feeling vulnerable and fragile, and will find it hard to see themselves in a positive light. The most beautiful thing you can do for them is to provide a solid, loving presence that isn't conditional on the way they think, feel or act, or on how quickly they get better.

Love: what does it look like?

If patient love is a profound blessing, what does it actually look like?

The beauty of love is that it can manifest itself in so many ways.

It could be an invitation to a cafe, a sporting field, or a church. It could be a home-cooked meal. It could be the gift of a book or movie. It could be a word of encouragement, or it could be to choose to say nothing at all. Over time, you will learn in what specific ways you can be a blessing in the life of another.

In whatever form it takes, be *consistent*.

If you bond over coffee, have coffee when the person is struggling and when they're not. The same can be said for a gift or an act of service. Pop round with flowers when your friend is feeling good as well as when they're not. Invite them to join you for a walk because it's a lovely day rather than only when you are worried about them. Your loved one may not always take you up on the offer, but that isn't the point. That act of love isn't about them serving you; it's about you serving them. And quite possibly the best way you can do that is to demonstrate your love for them in all seasons. Don't just do this with words, but show it in action as well.

> *A friend loves at all times, and a brother is born for a time of adversity.* PROVERBS 17 V 17

Care for the carer

When I came out of hospital, one of the first things I realised was that the past couple of years had taken their toll on Lara, my wife. She had been my primary caregiver every day under very difficult circumstances.

If you're caring for a loved one, please know that you're allowed to be affected by what's happening around you. You, as the carer, need to be cared for also. That care will need to come from a third party—a pastor, a psychologist or a trusted friend. Why? Because the one you're caring for won't likely be able to reciprocate the same level of care for you.

Talking to someone you trust about how you're coping will be important for you. You will also need to keep the boundaries around confidentiality clear, so that you can talk about what's happening with your loved one without any risk that rumours will be spread.

In my time in pastoral ministry, I have often seen that those who have strong empathy for others are also those who find it difficult to get help themselves. I believe this is because being someone's rock can easily turn into an adopted identity. Wonderfully, for Christians this needn't be the case. Your primary identity is as *a child of God* and recipient of his loving grace. So if you're struggling in your role as a carer, it doesn't reduce who you are in Christ, and you are allowed to get help.

While it's right and good that we care for others with patient love, sharing life with a loved one living with depression or anxiety will take an emotional and physical toll. Remember when that happens, that you're allowed to go to God, and use the resources he has placed in your life for your own support.

For reflection

What does patient love look like in your own context and relationships? Who can you call on for support for yourself?

CONCLUSION
MOTIVATION

Who are you?

As we conclude this journey together, my hope and prayer is that you've seen how faith in Christ can have a profound impact on your journey with depression, anxiety, or any other mental illness.

We've covered a lot of ground. How do we make sense of what's happening? Can we be healed? How do we pray? What about psychologists, medication and Christian community?

Under all these questions, hopefully you've seen the deeper question:

Who are you?

If the answer is "I don't know", then the temptation is to give up—disillusioned and hopeless. Life can become meaningless and all too hard.

But a person who has a deeper purpose—a deeper identity—has a framework to help them persevere. This is true for us as Christians. *Who are you?* Your identity is in Christ, and you're loved by God, who you worship each and every day.

Who you are will impact what you do.

And what can you offer?

In their Gospel accounts, both Mark and Luke write about a simple and yet profound event in Jesus' life.

> *Jesus sat down opposite the place where the offerings were put and watched the crowd putting their money into the temple treasury. Many rich people threw in large amounts. But a poor widow came and put in two very small copper coins, worth only a few pence [cents].*
>
> *Calling his disciples to him, Jesus said, "Truly I tell you, this poor widow has put more into the treasury than all the others. They all gave out of their wealth; but she, out of her poverty, put in everything—all she had to live on.*   MARK 12 V 41-44

Jesus' observations are both shocking and stunning. Shocking, because everyone else is justifying themselves by exterior performance. And stunning, because once again we're reminded of God's compassionate, loving heart.

Emotionally speaking, you may have just two copper coins to give on any given day. To everyone else, your life may look unimpressive. Others may wonder what's happened to you. They may even pass judgment. But consider the message of the widow—Christ has such compassion on his children. Honour him with what you have, whether it's much or little.

You may spend your two coins by getting out of bed tomorrow morning and having a shower. You could spend them in five minutes of prayer. Or perhaps it's making an appointment with a psychologist for the very first time. But know that even with two coins—especially with two coins—your opportunities to worship the one who loves you are significant. Slowly and surely, your reserves will build, and with that increased currency your purpose remains the same—to love and worship the one who has given you everything, not least of all life itself.

You are loved.

FOR FURTHER HELP

There are a number of support networks for those whose lives are at risk from depression or anxiety. In my experience, it's easy for us to downplay just how bad things are in our own minds, and so I firmly encourage you to seek help, even if you don't think it's entirely necessary. To use the old adage, it's better to be safe than sorry.

Australia

- **Beyond Blue**—1300 22 46 36, www.beyondblue.org.au

- **Emergency Services** (Ambulance)—dial 000

- **Kids' Help Line**—1800 55 1800, https://kidshelpline.com.au

- **Lifeline**—13 11 14, www.lifeline.org.au

- **MensLine Australia**—1300 78 99 78, https://www.mensline.org.au

- **Suicide Call Back Service**—1300 659 467,
  www.suicidecallbackservice.org.au

- **Black Dog Institute**—
  https://www.blackdoginstitute.org.au

- **Headspace**—https://www.headspace.org.au/
  (includes an online chat feature for immediate
  counselling)

UK

- **Association of Christian Counsellors**—
  https://www.acc-uk.org

- **MIND**—0300 123 3393, https://www.mind.org.uk

- **Samaritans**—116 123, https://www.samaritans.org

- **Childline**—0800 1111, https://www.childline.org.uk

- **Emergency Services**—dial 999

USA

- **National Suicide Prevention Lifeline**—
  1-800-273-8255, https://suicidepreventionlifeline.org

- **Kristin Brooks Hope Center**—
  https://www.imalive.org

- **Psychology Today** referral system for therapists,
  psychiatrists, and support groups near you—
  https://therapists.psychologytoday.com/rms

- **Veterans Peer Support Line**—1-877-838-2838

- **Spanish-Speaking Suicide Hotline**—1-800-784-2432

- **Teen to Teen Peer Counseling Hotline**—1-877-968-8454

- **Grad Student Hotline**—1-800-472-3457

- **Postpartum Depression Hotline**—
  1-800-773-6667

- **Emergency Services**—dial 911

END NOTES

1. (page 18) "Desert Song", words & music by Brooke Ligertwood © 2008 Sony/ATV Music Publishing Australia (AUS & NZ only), Hillsong Music Publishing (rest of world).

2. (page 41) *The Table Talk or Familiar Discourse of Martin Luther*, translated by W. Hazlitt, (London, 1848).

THANK YOU

To my Lord and Saviour, I love you. While I wouldn't wish my journey upon anyone, I pray that you continue to use me for your glory and kingdom.

To Lara, I love you. When we made our vows, we knew it wouldn't always be easy. But it's a joy and privilege to go on this journey of life with you—in sickness and in health. Thank you for walking with me.

To Ella, Grace, Louis and Josephine, I love you and pray that you follow Jesus all of your days. I hope that when you're old enough to understand, you'll be proud of your dad. You'll one day realise I'm not invincible, and you'll learn that God's power is made perfect in weakness.

To Mum and Dad, I know this all probably came out of nowhere for you, but thank you for the foundations you built in my life. Your love and acceptance of me has helped me to love and accept myself.

To Rob, thank you for showing me that grace and truth win out over condemnation and guilt. You have restored my faith in the power of unconditional love in God's church. Some of what you have taught me has been in what you *say*. Most of what you have taught me has been in who you *are*.

And to Alison, thank you for taking a chance on an unknown Australian pastor with a story to tell. Your prayers for me, and the readers of this book, have meant so much. I can't wait to see how God uses it to bless many who walk the journey that we do. He is working mightily through you.

SUFFERING IS REAL. BUT SO IS HOPE.

This is a book for those who are going through a time of struggle, or who love someone who is. A book for women who feel perplexed, defeated, struck down, abandoned or despairing. A book written by two women who are walking through these times themselves. A book that gives hope—because God wants to give us hope not just beyond our hurts, but in our hurts.

thegoodbook.co.uk/hope | thegoodbook.com/hope

HOW TO REPLACE ANXIETY WITH PEACE

We all worry. Some of us worry all the time, some of us worry some of the time; but we all know what anxiety is.

This book is written by a man who has helped countless anxious people to find real peace. He will not give you easy answers or a trite "six steps to know peace"; but he will give you real answers, and a way to face your anxieties and pursue real joy. If you ever worry, you will want to read this book.

thegoodbook.co.uk/worry | thegoodbook.com/worry

thegoodbook
COMPANY

BIBLICAL | RELEVANT | ACCESSIBLE

At The Good Book Company, we are dedicated to helping Christians and local churches grow. We believe that God's growth process always starts with hearing clearly what he has said to us through his timeless word—the Bible.

Ever since we opened our doors in 1991, we have been striving to produce resources that honour God in the way the Bible is used. We have grown to become an international provider of user-friendly resources to the Christian community, with believers of all backgrounds and denominations using our Bible studies, books, evangelistic resources, DVD-based courses and training events.

We want to equip ordinary Christians to live for Christ day by day, and churches to grow in their knowledge of God, their love for one another, and the effectiveness of their outreach.

Call us for a discussion of your needs or visit one of our local websites for more information on the resources and services we provide.

Your friends at The Good Book Company
